the
Fingerprints
of
God

the
Fingerprints
of
God

Seeing His Hand in the Unexpected

Nancy Hoag

Fleming H. Revell
A Division of Baker Book House Co
Grand Rapids, Michigan 49516

Published by Fleming H. Revell
a division of Baker Book House Company
P.O. Box 6287, Grand Rapids, MI 49516-6287

Printed in the United States of America

Library of Congress Cataloging-in-Publication Data

Hoag, Nancy, 1939–
    The fingerprints of God : seeing his hand in the unexpected / Nancy Hoag.
         p.   cm.
    ISBN 0-8007-5809-9
    1. Christian women—Religious life. I. Title.
    BV4527 .H615 2002
    242′.643—dc21   2002001775

Unless otherwise noted, Scripture quotations are from the HOLY BIBLE, NEW INTERNATIONAL VERSION®. NIV®. Copyright © 1973, 1978, 1984 by International Bible Society. Used by permission of Zondervan. All rights reserved.

Scripture marked KJV is from the King James Version of the Bible.

For current information about all releases from Baker Book House, visit our web site:
                        http://www.bakerbooks.com

Contents

Contents

Introduction

He makes me lie down in green pastures, he leads me
beside quiet waters, he restores my soul.

Psalm 23:2–3a

The psalmist tells me I was woven together in my
mother's womb . . . and so were you. Each of us was fear-
fully and wonderfully made. For most of us, however,
life soon became a struggle, often overwhelming. I don't
think I saw this more clearly than the day my husband
announced I would be moving again. We would be
vacating the home we'd taken months to build, the Montana home my husband had said we would live in as
long as we lived on this earth.

I'd been uprooted six times in seventeen years—and
that didn't include the motels and apartments we'd occupied while waiting for yet another home. Now—after
having lived in what, for me, had been a dream come
true—Scotty had been offered another promotion. We
would be leaving the land I loved. We'd be heading for
the agency's national headquarters, moving to the East
Coast again.

"I can't do it," I said. Not only was I trying to recu-
perate from a recent surgery, but every one of the pre-

ceding migrations had taken so much out of me. When we'd moved to this home from Pennsylvania, I hadn't been able to work for months. All my equipment—my computer, typewriter, printers, and disks—had gone into storage. Even my file folders and addresses for editors. Everything. Everything that made me feel like me.

It would be a three-day pack, the movers told us this time. They would begin with the glassware and the second floor.

"No, please, no," I whispered. Not the second floor. My office was up there—the office I'd prayed for, the miniature study under the eaves, with a view of the mountains, the pond, and the deer. Up there, I watched sunsets and speckled fawns and listened to newborn calves beyond a stand of cottonwood. And I wrote. I wrote in the morning and after lunch. I watched the seasons change in the meadow and delighted in winter's first snowfall and watched for the fox that frequented the spot out back where I'd planted two hundred flowering bulbs.

"Scotty," I pleaded.

"You can't go into her study," Scotty said to the movers, "until you're done with the garage and the rest of the house." He wrapped his arms around me. "She needs to work," he said.

I needed to work, but we both knew I wouldn't be working at all. I would be grieving, stalling, hiding from yet another gang of packers. I would be wondering about friendships I'd leave behind and doubting I had it in me to find more. I would be sorting through rough drafts and daydreams on paper and thinking my career was over, that this time I would completely shut down.

For two days I took meals in my study while Scotty supervised everything else in our home. I could hear the movers below, on the first floor, then in the bedroom next door.

The third day, they cleared the crawl space. They were digging deep in our garage. Nothing left, really, except the study where I was secluded.

Scotty had promised he wouldn't let them pack my computer and printers. He'd saved the boxes; he'd pack them himself. "But, Babe, it's time," he said. "We can't put them off any longer." The crew had other jobs to go to.

"Please. . . ." I needed just a few more minutes. "Please," I whispered again at the door. "Just give me a little more time." I'd been sitting on the carpet in the middle of the room. I'd been trying to hear God, believing he had blessed my husband but not blessed me. I had journals full of my words and pages where I'd noted God's as well. My morning devotions had all been recorded; I'd been trying for years to line up with his plan. Now we were moving? Now I was being asked to give it all up again?

"God!" I screamed—and I threw a devotional against my wall. "Why? Why . . . ?" This time, I threw a favorite Bible, then watched its pages pitch and tumble across my carpeted floor. "Not only are they going to pack up everything that identifies me; we have no place to go!" With no home at the other end, we didn't know where we'd be living. All our belongings, except for two suitcases of clothing and cosmetics, would go into an alien warehouse. I'd be staying in my youngest daughter's cellar. "I don't have a home anymore! I HAVE NO IDENTITY!" I cried. I slammed my fist on the wall—and heard my phone.

The woman at the other end sounded as if she were beside herself, too. I didn't recognize her voice. "Are you Nancy Hoag?" she was asking.

I tried to clear my throat, tried to talk. "I am," I finally managed, as the other woman began to weep. "Praise God, praise God," she said.

Praise God for what? I wondered.

"You don't know me," she was saying. "I'm a pastor's wife in Jackson, Ohio, and we were missionaries in Papua New Guinea for years—but I've never done *anything* like this."

She'd never done what?

"I was having my quiet time this morning," she continued without taking a breath, "and the devotion I was using had been written by you, and God spoke to me and said I was to find you." Now she was openly crying. "I don't know where you are or anything about your situation," she said.

The hair on my arms had begun to stand straight up; I felt a shiver wrap itself around me; my heart had grown still.

"But he told me I was to find you and that I was to give you a message."

The goose bumps traveled my body like fingers on piano keys. No words would come.

"So this is it," the obviously shaken woman was saying. "He wants me to tell you . . ." I heard tears catch in her throat. "He knows your name, and he knows your address." She paused as I gasped and started weeping.

My name? My address? I had nothing to put on a forwarding card. She couldn't have known; she couldn't have imagined. But God knew.

"You couldn't have known," I said—and then I listened—as she began to tell me that she'd felt afraid to make the call, but the Holy Spirit had spoken clearly to her. She'd felt foolish, but she'd known almost from the beginning that God wasn't going to accept her "No."

For the first time in weeks, my tears were joyful. What would happen at the other end of our winter drive? Would I write again? Would we find a home? Would editors wait while I pulled myself together, while I relocated my equipment and my files and figured out where to make copies and whether or not publishers even wanted what it was I had to say . . . and while I looked for and made another friend?

It no longer mattered; I'd not lost my identity. "I know your name," God had said. And though I hadn't yet seen it with my own eyes, he was preparing a place for us. "I know your address."

In this life, God explains in his Word, we can expect there will be troubles and tests. Many of us already know this from experience. The earth seems to have dropped away from beneath us, even as we've struggled to stand. We hear of wars and rumors of wars, and we long to turn the sound down. There are days when we don't completely understand, days when we don't know what God is doing until after the fact. Still, even when my feelings try to tell me otherwise, I am learning he is not only very much alive but he is for us. With my growing awareness that he really is watching, I am finally learning not only to draw near to him but to trust.

Come with me; I want to share with you stories that are true, stories that are mine, memories I cling to when I can no longer bear to hear or read the evening news. There may be days when you also feel as if everything you loved has been taken from you, nights when you will think it might be easier not to go on. I encourage you to find yourself a quiet place and a season in which to listen. I encourage you to walk with me through the pages that reveal where I have been, pages that make it clear that God was with me—and that he is also with you.

Part I

Why, Lord?

Then we will no longer be infants, tossed back and forth
by the waves, and blown here and there by every wind
of teaching and by the cunning and craftiness of men in
their deceitful scheming.

Ephesians 4:14

1

Hanging by a
Thinning Thread

Immediately Jesus reached out his hand and caught him.

Matthew 14:31a

Life is difficult, as many of us have both experienced and read. But it is fragile, too, as fragile as a thread. We get up in the morning expecting a glorious brand-new day, but then the phone rings, and the news isn't good. We send a child off to school believing we've prepared her for all that she'll face and the untruths the teachers will try to tell her, but then she comes home one day and tells us we don't understand, we're more than just a little old-fashioned, she has a new way of thinking now . . . a greater understanding. A baby is born, a mother holds him, but then the doctors say he isn't well, there is this problem.

I remember when I was trying to go to college as a young wife and mother and my doctor said "cancer" for the second time. After having surgery and taking one quarter off, I returned to my classes—and wondered if I would ever again feel the same about my life, my goals, my future.

I remember thinking, soon after my first husband remarried, that life would never again be anything like what I had expected. I tried to place the blame on someone else's shoulders, everyone else's shoulders actually. But there are two sides to every story, because we are human beings, flesh and blood—and fragile.

I remember driving by a house I hated to give up and seeing what appeared to be a happy family in the kitchen window. A happy family filling the home that once had been mine.

I remember many times—too many times—thinking God had simply forgotten me. He wasn't watching, no matter what I'd read in his Word—because there were so many people for him to watch, so many others in greater need, women who'd walked a straighter line, women who'd been more faith-filled. But then the phone would ring, and the voice of a friend—and on more than one occasion, a stranger—would say God had impressed them to call and that he would always be there for me. That he cared even more than I did, that he was faithful.

Last night, I sat alone on the deck and looked out over the mountains. The moon had filled the valley; just the hint of a sunset continued to perch on the western horizon. And God spoke. Not audibly, but as a still, small voice. He spoke to my heart as I sat and watched and thought I simply couldn't go to bed. I couldn't miss any of the night, couldn't bear to sleep when the world was quiet and there were whispers from the wind he had created. When I listened even more closely, I could hear the

16

wheat field out back. I could hear the grasses waltz and the nighthawk skim the sky in his quest for the evening meal that God had provided for him.

And I remembered being with my grandfather when I was no more than five or six years old. Or maybe I was seven. We'd gone to the lake where my aunt and uncle had a cabin. A lake . . . just the sound of the word, and the feel of it in my mouth makes me smile, because I have long been in love with the water. Married to a cowboy, I'm pretty much landlocked now, but where I grew up it seemed there was always a lake and a cabin. Anyway, this particular summer, we had gone to stay for several days and nights, and I'd experienced the joy—although I didn't yet know how to swim—of lying on my back in the shallow place with water wings or an inner tube beneath me.

One morning, however, the shallow water just wasn't enough. I wasn't a truly brave child, but I sometimes felt this sense of adventure grab me. That morning it grabbed, and I headed for the end of the dock. What could it hurt if I dangled my feet a little? Yes, my mother had said, "Don't you dare go where the water's deep," and my father had seconded her warning. But the sun was warm, and there were ducks out there, and if I got just a little ways out, I could look back and see the cabin and how big the sun looked in the trees.

At the end of the dock, dangling my feet for a little while was satisfying. Twenty or so minutes later, however, it was boring. Maybe if I just hung onto a piling and sort of dangled my whole self, I'd be safe. The pilings were strong but not very big around; I could wrap my arms tight and just sort of hang there.

So I did, and I remember feeling as if I'd suddenly grown up. Water all the way to my shoulders, water all around me. I liked it like that, and one day I was going to learn to swim, and then I'd go all the way to the middle of the lake, maybe farther.

Within minutes, however, hanging from the piling became as boring as when my feet had dangled. That's when I spotted the twine someone had attached to the underside of the wooden dock my uncle had built. That's when I decided I'd just do something even more fun. I'd reach for that twine, hang on tight, and float out flat on my back. Because I was only five or six or seven, I knew for a fact I was immortal. No, I wasn't supposed to be out here, and yes, my parents had warned me. But just for a few minutes? What could happen?

On my back, I felt more special than I'd ever felt in my life. Not only was the water giving me all of its support, the threadlike twine felt like thick rope in my hands, and I just knew that I could lie there—where they couldn't see me from the cabin—for almost as long as I wanted.

It was during this bragging to myself and my believing that no one could possibly see or scold me that the twine broke and I began to go under the water and under the weathered boards of the dock. With my mouth full of water and then my eyes, I was going down and up and down and—

That's when Grandpa caught me. I hadn't known he was there, I'd been so enamored with myself and all that sky and water. I hadn't heard him coming to the end of the dock for me, because I'd been listening to the way the waves lapped.

But he'd been there, and just about the time I began again to sink, with the thin thread still clutched between my fingers, he'd stretched out his hand and reached me. He held my hand tight, said, "You're okay," and then began to lift me up. Pretty soon my feet were on the dock beside my grandpa, and I was shivering not only from the cold lake but from the fear.

But Grandpa was smiling now and shaking his head and saying, "You are a rascal, you know that?" Watching his smile, I was so glad he was there. I was also glad because he was saying we didn't have to go telling the whole world that I had done this, but next time I needed to remember. And that's when I smiled back, because Grandpa wasn't going to suggest that I be given a spanking. He wasn't going to go back to that cabin and tell everyone that I had misbehaved—because my grandpa loved me, and he'd been watching, and he'd reached out his hand when his hand was what I needed. He could have come down that dock, shouting, "Nancy Grace! You get out of that lake!" But he'd given me the time to experience what I needed to experience. He'd let me see for myself just what that twine I'd trusted was made of.

Hanging by a thinning thread, that's what I'd been doing. And isn't that what we adults do sometimes? Don't we think, because we believe no one's seen or overheard us, that just maybe this once we might try something we should not try? Don't we often get ourselves into the deepest part of the water and then want to blame others or God? Don't we too often think this is the end, he doesn't care, that he's not even watching?

But Grandpa was, and so is God. Watching us, giving us a little more rope than we can handle . . . and then reaching out his hand and showing us how very much he cares and how very fragile the threads of our lives can be . . . without him.

This morning, sitting out on my deck and watching the sun rise on the mountains he created, I remembered again the lake and Grandpa. Drawing my robe around me, I knew that no matter how fragile life has seemed over the past several months, God is with me and for me.

And this God who has been watching and who loves me? If you'll let him, he'll reach out his hand to you, too, and draw you out of the place where you feel certain you are sinking. His heart is also toward you and the fears that you are feeling. He isn't going to go and tell the others how you are behaving or how disappointing you may have been to him.

I say these things without hesitation . . . because I have been there. I know that I know—no matter how we've misbehaved—he loves us. "Us" means me *and* you.

2

When You've Made a Big Splash—and They're Watching

If we're not allowed to laugh in heaven, I don't want to
go there.

Martin Luther

Have you ever said the wrong thing in public? Longed
to take back your words? If you have, you know how
difficult it can be to laugh at yourself. For most of my
life, I've found it nearly impossible to laugh at myself.
But God says in his Word, "A merry heart doeth good
like a medicine" (Prov. 17:22 KJV), and there is "a time
to laugh" (Eccles. 3:4b). I think it's possible he is saying
we might do well to laugh not just at a situation but at
ourselves.

Just the other day, a friend told me about a time when she was still a teen and doing her best to look not like twelve but twenty. She wanted to be "cool"—to have the boys think she was special. She'd gone to a rink to skate with older friends and had spent a great deal of time in the ladies' room checking out her outfit, daubing on a little lipstick, fixing and refixing her hair. But when she began again to glide into the skating circle—certain she'd make a spectacular impression—she heard one giggle and then another. Looking down, she discovered a train of white tissue clinging to one roller skate wheel and trailing behind her. "What could I do? I wanted them to think I was a good sport, so I laughed, too," she said.

As for me, when I've done something I wish I had *not* done—said the wrong thing at the wrong time, tripped, stumbled, fallen—I go back to fifth grade and the summer I learned to swim.

My sister and I had been taking lessons at the YWCA, but our parents had taken us to a city park. We girls would spend the afternoon in the pool while our parents would watch from the sidelines. Typically unsure of myself, I felt awkward at first as I'd walked across the concrete to the low dive. On the other hand, my swimming instructor had said I was doing super. Not only that, I had a brand-new swimsuit. A two-piece in yellow with leopard spots, and this particular afternoon I was feeling not nearly so knobby-kneed. Actually, it was one of those rare days when I was feeling kind of special.

The first one into the water was my sister. She'd gotten in, however, by sliding off the edge of the pool. I'd decided I would show off just a little, climb up on that diving board, wait for a chance to catch the eye of first one and then the other parent, so they could see just how brave a child I could be.

I'd waited long enough so the boys behind me had begun to make noises about my coming down now, but

I didn't want to come down. I wanted to dive, and I wanted my mother and father to notice. Pretending to be more self-assured than I felt, I folded my arms. Surely, before long, my parents would turn around and see.

Hooray! They *were* turning around. This was it, perfect timing. I ran to the end of the board, stretched tall on the tips of my toes just as my instructor had instructed, and shouted, "Watch *me!*" In my most perfect form, which wasn't perfect at all, of course, I dove and felt something awful happen. I'd pushed off just as my teacher had said I should, and I hadn't done a belly flop, but the top of my swimsuit had pushed off, too— only not with me! It had gone in first, and now I was flying through the air toward the water behind it!

I don't remember how long I stayed submerged in that pool. It wasn't that I couldn't find my suit; it was leopard in yellow and brown; it showed up like a boy shows up for lunch. No one could miss that swimsuit top, and it wasn't all that difficult to slip it back on with just my eyes and nose above the chlorine. So what took me so long? Mustering courage, yes, but also thinking everyone would be watching me surface, and then they would be laughing. But they weren't. Instead, they were jumping off the sides of the pool just as they had been doing when I went under, and it didn't take me long to figure out that no one but me—and my parents—had actually seen my swimsuit top go flying through the air.

Nothing much has changed since then. I still make mistakes, find myself in awkward spots, say words I should not say. In fact, several days ago, a friend asked how I could get over something I'd done, something that made me feel the fool for a moment. I told her that, over the years, I've discovered I'm often the only one who's even noticed. I recalled the week when I'd only just entered the eighth grade and a doctor said, "Corrective shoes." I had developed a problem not only with my feet but with one leg and my back, and when the salesman opened the box to show me the shoes, I thought I would die. Couldn't I have something prettier?

"No," the salesman said. Corrective shoes came only in brown with laces.

I'd be wearing shoes that looked like World War II? Fighting tears, I watched the man measure my feet. Tomorrow, I'd be back in school looking like a dope. Tomorrow, while the other girls paraded the halls in saddle shoes and sandals, I would feel like hiding. I would know my shoes were ugly. "They're all going to laugh," I'd started to say, when the salesman looked up.

"You smile your smile," he said, "and no one will look at your feet." He handed the second shoe to me. "They won't even know you're *wearing* shoes," he said.

And the following day? It turned out he was right. In fact, not once in all of the months wearing those awful brown shoes did anyone laugh.

So, on those self-conscious days when I've been disappointed or embarrassed myself? I sometimes laugh; I try always to smile; I remember that the whole world *isn't* taking notice . . . and while there may be laughter, they're *not* all laughing at me.

3

When You Think
You're Off-Course

Many are the plans in a man's heart, but it is the LORD's purpose that prevails.

Proverbs 19:21

Life in ninth grade can be traumatic and dramatic and crushing. Add to that a wishful longing and then the news that there'll be no dream coming true, and a girl could almost give up. I know, because I did. Almost.

"You won't be going to college," my ninth-grade advisor said. It didn't matter that I'd worked hard, that I'd earned nothing but A's and sometimes A+. My parents had no money. The man had been kind; he'd said he knew I had it in my heart and head to be going with the others, but he'd advised lots of kids, and he knew what he knew. "We'll sign you up for the business courses," he said. At least I'd have a way to feed and clothe myself and keep a roof over my head.

I wanted to tell him I could play the piano and I wrote and that I'd always loved to study. I wanted to be an Interior Decorator or a Home Economist or sing beautiful songs on stage. I'd work hard; I'd get a part-time job; I'd do whatever I needed to do.

My advisor shook his head. "Business courses," he repeated, taking out the schedule of classes they'd be offering at the secondary school.

So, while my friends who earned C's all enrolled in higher math and Latin, I signed up for typing and, because my advisor said I should, I also marked the box they'd labeled "Shorthand." I wouldn't be joining a sorority; I wouldn't be packing my bags and crossing the state with the others. I'd be staying in my own neighborhood to work first in a shipyard and then for an airplane manufacturer.

I would also marry, I decided only three years after my advisor's pronouncement. Why not? There was nothing really to look forward to; everyone I knew from junior high and high school would be going in an entirely different direction. Not until my marriage began to fall apart, however, did I understand that—from the time of my birth and even before—the God I'd come to know at the age of fifteen had been watching.

"College," I said, one day over coffee with another young wife and mother. I wanted to go; I wanted to try. Two of my children attended elementary school, and my third and youngest would stay several hours a day with a favorite neighbor. I wanted to get my degree, the one I'd dreamed about even before I'd entered kindergarten.

And that's what I did. I went to college as a young mother and with things not going very well at our house. Though he was reluctant to do so, the dean decided he would grant me permission to take twenty-three credits at a time; he understood, after I explained it to him, that I needed to get as much schooling as I could for the money I'd be spending.

"You really shouldn't do this, though," a counselor told me in his office one day. "You'll burn out; it's too many classes for you with all you have going at home." But I'd been here before and had heeded advice I hadn't wanted to hear; I knew where I needed to go and what I would need to get there. I knew I needed these classes and that I would study all night if I had to. I also knew there would be one thing working in my favor. Make that two. I knew how to type, and I took shorthand. Though I had lists in my purse reminding me not to forget the groceries I'd need to pick up after school each day, and there'd be ironing to do in the morning and children to see to and a house to keep up, I could make it if I took down every single word my professors spoke in each classroom. I could make it if I waited for my children to fall asleep, because then I could type my elaborate notes and read and reread until I understood completely. The typing and the shorthand hadn't been a mistake after all; they'd become what I was beginning to see as a strength.

It took me just three years to earn my first degree— going straight through during the summer and taking only one quarter off for a surgery my doctor said I needed. And at the end of those three years, when my husband took an apartment and, soon after, remarried, I was offered financial help to continue my education. It would mean, for me, a decent salary.

At first, I was telling myself, "You'll never be able to do this." But I *was* able. I would take shorthand notes during class, run back to student housing, retrieve my daughter from the neighbor's house, feed her, prepare her for the evening, go to my waitressing job, and, after I returned home, transcribe my notes—which I could do quickly, because I'd also taken all that typing. It wasn't some trick my ninth-grade advisor had played. I was going to need every one of those business courses; I was going to need them in a way I hadn't been able to comprehend when I was turning thirteen.

Often, life is like that. We think that we know the way we should go. We have our dreams and our goals, and we're thinking we have the right stuff to get there. But sometimes we don't. Often we don't. Only God knows for certain what we'll need and what we won't. In my ninth-grade year, he knew I'd need typing and shorthand. Not just for college or to feed myself, but later, as well, when he called me to write and not to teach. Later, when I would attend writers' conferences during the day and take care of a home at night and bake and sew on buttons and cook something decent for a meal. Later, when a deadline would make its way to my desk calendar, and there was research to do, and my limited time meant I couldn't get it all down and together—without the shorthand.

The Word says, "Many are the plans in a man's heart" (Prov. 19:21), and for years there were many in mine. But today? Today, I trust that God knows exactly what I need and where I'm going. Today, I write articles and books because I've given my dreams to him and because he is in the lead.

I've finally been able to let go . . . because he is and was always faithful . . . all the way back to when I was thirteen and even before. God—not my ninth-grade advisor—saw to it that I received all the training and all the necessary courses. Shorthand brought my head above the water; typing was the way I stayed afloat.

God in the beginning and in the end.

God who is always for and not against us.

The God who keeps us on course and whose purposes prevail.

4

I Remember Joan

A man's pride brings him low, but a man of lowly spirit gains honor.

Proverbs 29:23

Last night a former classmate called, one I hadn't talked to in more than thirty years; but it could have been just yesterday the way we carried on, remembering days of daring and recalling how clever we'd imagined ourselves to be. Had we really believed we would make life go our way? Well, it hadn't. There'd been difficult times and surprises without joy in them and far fewer answers than questions for my friend and for me.

"As smart as we were, we didn't know much, did we?" Cathy laughed.

"Not much," I said. "Although I did learn a couple of important lessons in our senior year." I'd learned them because of a girl named Joan.

To borrow a phrase from the fifties, "bosom buddies" Joan and I were not. I ran with a sassier, more visible crowd. On stage and full of ourselves, my friends and I treated Joan like we might a prop. Daily after school, I could be found with a microphone in one hand and a song on my *Tangee* lips—while Joan faced a piano in a corner so dingy not even her own mother could pick her out.

Because we frequently sang in churches, my partner Patty and I pretended our singing was "a ministry." But the real truth? We'd have done just about anything for a chance to wear high heels, taffeta, and *Evening in Paris* perfume. Worse, when anyone from the school or local paper happened by, we'd flutter our over-curled lashes and don humble faces—all for the love of recognition. Meanwhile, music tucked under her arm, Joan would tag along and sit at the upright to play like an angel, while Patty and I preened and bowed.

In the beginning, our duo performed only in informal settings and only close to home. One day, however, we were invited by a group of senior citizens to perform in a well-known hall across town. This was big time; they were going to pay us a bunch! Still, sharing a Studebaker's backseat and a ride into the city, Patty and I had more than money on our minds. Yes, we were anticipating an eager audience and an honorarium large enough for a crinoline or two, but this particular evening, our gossip centered on the upcoming prom, dates with the neatest guys on campus, strapless gowns, and permission to ride in a football letterman's car.

Focused entirely on ourselves, we said nothing to Joan. How could she understand what we were talking about? While we spent hours poring over *Seventeen* and *Photoplay*, didn't Joan read her Bible at home? Saturdays, while Patty and I painted our nails orange and dreamed about snagging some Ace in white bucks, didn't

Joan help her mother bake for some dumb function for the church or Sunday school? No, boys weren't Joan's thing; she just wouldn't be interested in any talk about the prom.

We'd been at our secretive chatter for nearly half-an-hour when, nearing our destination, Patty gave me one of her looks, and I gave her one of mine. We'd talk about the boys and the dance later, we were saying. Then, swishing into the auditorium like two clones of Loretta Young, we donned our grins and began the business of charming while completely ignoring Joan.

We'd performed for nearly an hour, and now we were twirling our poodle skirts toward the door—with the honorarium clutched in my sweaty palm—when an elderly woman with blue hair and pink cheeks began to sing, "Girls, wait! We're holding the drawing now."

Patty stared at me, and I stared back. What could they give away that would interest us? "Drawing?" We made a face for Joan.

"Why yes! We're giving away a door prize, and I've entered your names." The grandmother woman held high what looked like a man's fishing hat and shook it up while Patty wrinkled her nose and I wrinkled mine, too. We had *boys* to discuss. Why would we stay for some old drawing? We might have said so, too, if our pianist hadn't whispered, "Please, you guys, it won't take long." The look on her face told us she really meant, "Please, *please* don't be rude."

So we stayed. First on one irritated foot and then another, all the while tittering behind the double door.

"I don't know what I'm going to do with my hair," Patty groaned, running her fingers through her strawberry curls.

"I sure hope Diane will help me do something with my mop," I lamented, tightening the hot pink ribbon around my black bob.

31

"Wouldn't you just love to go to a beauty parlor that has a *French* name?" Patty sighed her most theatrical sigh.

"Golly, I only *wish* I could have mine styled," I groaned, imagining how cute a Bunny Wave could be.

"I wish I could have mine done, too," Joan peeped, suddenly beside us.

"Have *yours* done?" Patty blurted.

"For what?" I demanded, whipping my head sideways to look directly at Joan.

"For the prom," our pianist managed, her face fully flushed now.

"*You're* going to the prom?" we chorused.

"Yes," she said, but just barely.

"Well, we didn't think . . . I mean *you?*" Patty scrunched her freckled forehead.

"With whom?" I challenged.

"Yes," Patty said, her nose in the air, "I want you to tell *me*, too."

We'd have continued the inquisition, if our hostess hadn't placed a fingertip to her lips with, "Shush, the drawing's about to begin."

Meanwhile, Patty had eyed her Bulova, and I'd just checked mine when we heard the emcee sing, "Joan!"

"Who?" Patty mumbled. "What?" I croaked. But no one was looking at us.

"You've won, dear!" our hostess exclaimed, pushing past Patty to hug our piano player.

"It's all yours," a second fragile woman declared, as someone with a Polaroid snapped our pianist's picture and jostled me around. Then while Patty and I watched with our eyes and mouths open wide, Joan received her prize: the one and only gift certificate for the one and only complete hair styling at the finest *French* salon in town.

Today, there are mornings when I feel as if I've been out of high school forever and seasons when it's difficult to remember my hair wasn't always the color of snow. But last night, as I concluded the telephone conversation with Cathy, I realized I'd never forget the really important lessons I'd learned in my senior year—lessons about Joan's kind of giving, lessons about humility.

Today, women meet in my home for Bible studies because I've discovered how good it can feel to serve—even when that serving involves baking early in the morning and seeing to it coffee's not only hot but fresh-ground. Today, I've found out for myself how satisfying it is to reach out to neighbors. I've realized the thrill of sharing words that encourage. I know the joy of standing back while applause is given to another. Today, as I prepare the chocolate fudge cake and the table, I remember Joan.

5

My One and Only Trophy

We have different gifts, according to the grace given us.
. . . If it is serving, let him serve; if it is teaching, let him
teach.

Romans 12:6–7

No one who knows me well would call me athletic; no
one who knows me well would want me on their soft-
ball, basketball, or skiing team. No one who knows me
well believes it when I tell them I have on my desk a trophy. One I won for bowling. But I do have such a trophy; I have it because I did what I was supposed to do
while the other members of our team did what they did
best, too.

In the beginning, I was simply looking for a morning
out of the house. I had a preschooler to entertain; a
friend said that where she bowled they provided babysit-
ting. There'd be a glass partition; I could see my child,
and she could see me.

I asked where I could sign up. It would mean coffee in the company of women who spoke more than two-syllable words! Fellowship! A little bit of exercise—and, of course, just a little—was all I really wanted. I could wear a shirt like the shirts they wore; I'd belong somewhere, feel as if I'd joined the ranks of the jocks. In high school, the choir director made it possible for me to miss most of the physical education classes. It wasn't that I couldn't jump or run; I just didn't like doing such things in a gymnasium, when there was a piano to play. The director had worked it out for me to spend most of my day in the music wing of the school. I'd accompany the choir and ensembles and leave the volleyball, basketball, and gym suits to the girls who had it together. Now, however, friends had actually invited *me* to join their bowling team?

I hadn't bowled five minutes when I discovered the motive behind the invitation. "Your handicap," my closest friend on the bowling team said. It seemed their scores were so high, they needed me for a balance. Something about my doing gutter balls and throwing the ball behind me. Something having to do with their bowling in the high two-hundreds while my scores came in somewhere around forty-two. I didn't understand completely, and I'll admit I did feel a little bit embarrassed when they'd congratulate and cheer me on for my low score. But I was having fun all the same, and I could see my little girl through the glass partition, and she was having the time of her life, too.

Halfway through the season, I'd begun to record higher scores; several days I made it to the fifties and sixties. "I'm improving!" I'd cheer, delighted with my progress, wishing my teammates would look and sound more delighted, too. One day, I even bowled a near-two-hundred game. This called for a celebration! Maybe I'd become an athlete after all, instead of some bookworm who could only play the piano or, on occasion, teach a variety of classes for children. Maybe one day I'd even bowl a perfect score. I'd make that my goal, and at the end of the season, I was going to have my very own trophy.

The end of the season came in June, the same week the announcement was made that they'd be holding a Vacation Bible School at our church again this year, and I'd been "volunteered."

"You've always done this," the VBS director said. "You're good with the kids; you know you can teach." And hadn't I sort of hinted earlier that I'd be here?

"This isn't fair!" I said, as my teammates and I took off our bowling shoes and prepared to pick up our kids. "I'm going to have to tell them I can't, I will not, teach again this year." After all, we'd done so well all season that we were actually going to be included in a tournament. There was the very real possibility that we'd actually place or even come out on top. Though I'd only once bowled the near-two-hundred game—and even though the alley manager had warned that I was *not* to lob the ball behind me again—I'd really gotten into this sporting thing! My family was going to be so impressed!

"You go teach," I heard Darlene say, as I tied up my street shoes.

"Teach?" I couldn't have heard her correctly; I was a part of this team; they couldn't bowl with just three members. What would they do if I didn't show?

"We'll get a substitute for you," another member of our team said.

A substitute? Surely she was kidding; she knew how much this meant to me. And what about my trophy?

"It's your handicap," Darlene tried explaining. They would now select a better bowler as my replacement; this was going to give them a great advantage. Not only did I not understand why, but how disappointing not to see my name engraved, not to be part of a team of winners.

"So," I said, hoping I didn't sound like a kid about to cry. "I should tell them I'll teach?"

Darlene nodded; the others nodded, too.

That afternoon I called the church. I'd "sort of" volunteered at least nine months ago, I told them, so I guessed I'd follow through. I didn't tell them I'd rather be bowling; I just said I'd be there, asked them when the teachers would be meeting, said yes I'd taught both VBS and Sunday school for several years now, and I'd be happy to help out. I didn't say I'd be happier with a bowling trophy.

Two weeks later, children began to pour into my classroom; our Vacation Bible School was about to begin. I glanced at the clock; the bowling tournament was about to begin, as well. Darlene and the others would be meeting with my replacement while I would be sitting in a short-seated wooden chair. I'd be singing with children and introducing them to Moses and Jesus and Job on flannel boards and coloring lively pictures. I'd be playing the piano and then a drum and marching around a room with my brood lined up like baby chicks, each of them also pounding on something, each of them obviously happy to be here.

"We're so glad you agreed to teach," our leader said in the middle of the second morning. "You've done a great job," she added, as we neared the end of the week.

I didn't know about the "great" job, but I did admit by the end of the fifth day that I was glad I'd taught. I was glad when I watched the faces of children who'd come to understand not only who Jesus was but that he loved them. I was glad when I knelt by first one child and then another to offer a hug and to give them the gifts they'd made for their moms and dads; I was glad when I heard the voices of "my" children in a sing-along in the sanctuary. I wasn't glad, however, that I'd missed out on the one opportunity I would have for an award at the annual bowling celebration. I wasn't glad when I thought about the substitute person, the one who would no doubt have her name on the trophy I'd hoped would be mine. I wasn't glad, that is, until the director of VBS came into my room, just as the last child was leaving.

"There's a telephone call for you," she said.

A telephone call? Was something wrong at home?

She shook her head; she didn't think so; she thought the call was from a friend—one who sounded "ecstatic."

In the pastor's office with the receiver to my ear, I heard Darlene's voice. "We took 'Second Place'!" she sang, her announcement a mix of disbelief and joy. She hadn't actually thought we'd win; she'd only hoped. "But we did it! And the 'we' means you, too!"

"Me?" I asked. How was *that* possible? I'd been crawling around on my hands and knees with children; I'd been finger painting; I'd been teaching classes with one eye on the clock and my mind on what was going on at that bowling alley.

"Her handicap," Darlene said, and then she began to explain again what I would never understand. This time it wasn't just that I was not athletic or that many of my bowling balls never made it down the alley. It seemed the woman who was doing the substituting also had a low average. However, the team "just had this feeling" about her, and it had paid off. She'd not only bowled well, she'd bowled her highest game just when that highest score was needed.

The following week, the sponsors held a luncheon for all the bowlers in our league, and I was given my trophy. Not because I had bowled, but because I had not.

Today—after more than thirty years—that marble and bronze award still sits on a shelf above my desk. On top, there's a woman wearing a bowling shirt and shoes. On the base, it states that I was a part of the "Ladies Spring Trio" and that I was given this memento for taking second place. To me, however, it says something else. It reminds me that in that other setting, I had been a handicap; but in a classroom surrounded by children, I taught.

On a June morning in 1969, I was awarded my one and only trophy not for bowling but for teaching Vacation Bible School—because, in this life, it's all about fitting in where God decides, using the tools and talents he has given us.

It's about agreeing to do what we do best . . . what *he* has created each of us to do.

6

Fudge

By perseverance the snail reached the ark.

Charles Haddon Spurgeon

I don't remember their ages, but my children were young and short enough that the littlest had to have her feet planted on a chrome and vinyl chair to reach the kitchen counter.

It was almost Christmas; the baking had begun, and we were going to make our favorite fudge. Fudge for gifts and fudge enough to treat ourselves. We were all going to have a literal hand in the stuff with directions spread out on the counter for everyone, along with aprons and spoons.

Because they both knew how to read, my two oldest were given their assignments and a measure of independence, and things were actually going along pretty well. Tammy had melted the chocolate; Lisa would be adding the teaspoon of vanilla; Robbie, in the middle, had been put in charge of measuring the salt and chopped pecans. Not until it was time for the tasting, did we realize we had an emergency. We knew it when Lisa shouted, "Yuck!"—and then she made a sort of gagging sound with feeling and for a special effect.

Yuck? I looked first at Lisa and then at Tammy, too.

"Mom, this is *disgusting,*" my oldest was announcing now.

I grabbed a spoon, did my own tasting, and puckered up my own mouth. "Salt," I managed to spit out, feeling my throat constrict and going for a glass of water.

"I read the directions." Robbie didn't look happy; it wouldn't be the first time the girls had made him the object of their scorn.

But the girls hadn't created the problem for him this time. This time, he'd read the directions all by himself. So what in the world had gone wrong?

Within seconds, I had my answer. One-fourth teaspoon was what the recipe had called for but, for reasons none of us understood, my son had read one *and* one-fourth.

I looked at the faces of my disappointed children; they'd worked hard; they'd anticipated a sweet feasting. There was nothing to do but to take off our aprons, back out the station wagon, and head for the store.

Back home with bags full of chocolate, sugar, vanilla, and nuts and with my calculator telling me just how much of each ingredient I would need, we gathered every pan in the house—including the one I used for making soup and canning. Then we began the tedious business of adding to the concoction we'd first created.

That evening we not only dined on the fruits of our perseverance, but we filled boxes and tins of candy for nearly every friend in and outside of our neighborhood. We'd become a "Fudge Company," I later told a neigh-

41

bor over coffee. We'd created gifts for nearly everyone we knew.

Just a silly incident in the lives of three kids and their mom? Maybe. On the other hand, for me it has also served as a sweet reminder. When I became a single mom and was trying to earn an advanced degree while working at whatever job I could find, there was often a bitter taste in my mouth. Later, when my new husband's promotions relocated us repeatedly and forced me to pull up roots again and again, those relocations frequently seemed bitter experiences, as well. When teaching began to overwhelm me because classrooms had grown larger and I'd grown older, I fought the longings to quit.

But in each of these experiences, I learned some things. First, we can trash all that we've accomplished, or we can take stock of our situation and regroup. Second, we can determine where the recipe for our living has run amuck and make changes, or we can simply give up.

It hasn't always been easy; the older I get, the more I realize nothing is. But throw away what's good and sweet because a situation has introduced too little sugar and too much salt?

Nope, not me; I don't think so. I'm holding out for the fudge.

7

When You're Certain There Won't Be Enough

Your Father knows what you need before you ask him.

Matthew 6:8b

I'd become not only a single mother but a student again, and the money was so tight I'd taken a job carrying local papers. I'd also started working nights waiting tables to supplement the monthly $100.00 I would receive for child support. We could make it, I'd said, when a friend wrote to ask. The newspaper delivering wasn't going so well, though, because people would move out before they'd pay up. I'd expected only a pittance for an income, but now there was almost nothing at all. The waitressing job was another story. People were more generous than I'd previously believed them to be. Mention my child and my going to school, and the next thing you

43

knew, there was nearly as much left in tips as the weekly wage I would collect.

Still, with books to buy not just for me but for my daughter, when the subject of school clothes came up, I began to think we weren't actually going to stay afloat. We'd take a walk along Main Street, peer into windows, and talk about how much I'd like to buy a dress and stockings and a coat for her, but then I'd explain why I couldn't. "I'm sorry, honey," I'd say, "but I just don't have enough money."

"That's okay," she'd say, squeezing my hand. It didn't really matter anyway, because she "really liked" what she already had. She knew, of course, and so did I, that her dresses were growing too short, and the coveralls and denims were becoming threadbare, but she'd just bounce along with her hand in mine, and we'd go buy an ice-cream cone and sit on a bench to watch the traffic. Some nights, she would also pray, "Maybe I could have new clothes"—her head bowed and her eyelids scrunched tight, while I'd kneel down beside her. "Maybe," I'd say, echoing not only my daughter's request but trying also to echo her faith in the God who didn't seem to be there.

It was the morning after I'd bussed tables until after midnight that I learned God does hear a child's prayers—and supplies our every need—even when we least expect it.

I was running late. I had an early class and couldn't afford to be late, so I'd walked my little girl only halfway to her yellow bus. I could see her from where I was standing: The driver was coming down South Third; I waved, and my daughter waved back. Then I turned toward the university to begin the run toward the building where I would catch up with my instructor's morning harangue. I wasn't into this today; I was tired of carrying dishes to tables and back again to kitchens. I'd grown weary of putting up with a foul-tempered cook and with the occasional customer who made demands on those days when I had my daughter on my mind as well as some upcoming final exam.

"It's too much," I said, feeling on the verge of tears but sharing jokes with members of my class. They were making a place for me where I could not only hear every word our professor spoke but where I could also catch a glimpse of already-scribbled notes. I couldn't deny I was blessed with fellow students who understood that being a mom wasn't exactly a piece of cake. "And waiting tables?" one had said. "I don't know how you do it."

I'd shrugged the last time anyone had said such a thing, but this morning I was at the end of my strength. Last night's walk in front of the department store had done it for me. In the window there'd been a display of school clothes—including a plaid dress and a tiny denim coat. My daughter had smiled, but I had not. I knew she longed for new things, knew I couldn't buy them. God was watching, one friend had said. He would provide all of our needs, another had reminded. But brand-new clothes for a little girl whose mother carried papers and waited table?

That night, as I walked toward the bus and my daughter bounded from the stairs in a run and laughing, I discovered that my friends were right: God *is* watching, and he *does* provide.

"Mama! Mama!" Lisa began to sing. "Look what I found!" From her book bag, she pulled out a folded envelope and from that envelope just one bill. One marked "Twenty Dollars."

"Lisa, where—?"

"I found it by the bus stop!" she sang. She'd just started to board the bus when she saw something white in the grass. She'd bent over and picked it up about the time I'd turned around to make the dash to my class.

She'd found it? It was ours? Hers? "No," I said, shaking my head, because it wasn't. "It belongs to someone," I said, kneeling down beside her. "They might be feeling so bad right now; they might really need this money." *Like us*, I didn't say, but I was thinking.

"We can't keep it?" Lisa looked as if she would cry.

"No, honey," I said, hugging her tight. "We'll need to call someone."

"The police?" My daughter stood up straight and looked so grown-up.

"The . . . the police," I said, realizing she was right; that's who we'd call. There was no identification, not even a slip of paper in the envelope.

It took only minutes to walk back to student housing, and then I made the call, said my daughter had found some money, asked if they wanted me to bring it in.

"Nope," the man at the other end said. "You just hang onto it a while, watch the papers to see if anyone puts an ad in." Meanwhile, if anyone called the department to say they'd lost money and knew the amount and also that the envelope was plain white, we'd return the money to them. "Give it one week," the man said. "If no one calls, it's yours."

"It's ours?"

"Yup."

"Just like that?" It didn't seem right.

"Happens all the time," he said.

"Not to us," I wanted to say. "Okay," I said, instead—and we began the watch. Every night after school, we'd borrow the neighbor's paper and look through the *Lost and Found*—but not once, in seven days, did we see an ad for the money or hear back from the police.

The end of our wait came on a Wednesday morning.

"Today?" Lisa asked as she jumped out of bed.

"Today," I said. "Right after school." If she came home and no one had called, we'd shop. "*If* no one calls," I said again.

And no one did, and right after school, we walked into the department store. Much to our surprise, while we'd been watching the *Lost and Found,* all the prices on kids' clothes had been marked down. It was an end-of-the-month sale or something. I don't honestly know. All I can clearly recall is that my daughter, with a big grin on her face, danced from rack to rack. Picking one of these and one of those. Shopping like a professional, looking at price tags, asking if I thought this one was pretty or should she buy something else instead. Since the prices had been slashed several times, we filled not just one bag but two. We filled them with play pants, blouses, shirts, and socks, and even a blue bandana she would tie around her neck "Because I really like that," she said, bobbing from one display to the next.

Walking home that night, with each of us carrying a shopping bag, we talked about what "my girl" would pick out for school tomorrow. And I knew at last that God was watching. Not only that, he'd known what we would need even before we'd asked. He knew we would need twenty dollars *and* a period of waiting . . . while a department store prepared for a sale that would fill not just one shopping bag but two . . . and give a little girl her brand-new plaid dress *and* her tiny denim coat.

8

Any Which Way
but Down

If the Lord delights in a man's way, he makes his steps firm.

Psalm 37:23

This would be my first ski season, but I'd married a Montanan who'd skied nearly all of his life. Worse, he'd worked as a professional ski patroller, and now he headed up the volunteer patrol—with more than one old girlfriend volunteering as well. So I'd made up my mind; I was going to learn to ski if it was the last thing I did. And one day I would also do what the others did—climb 600 vertical feet above the highest lift and ski from "The Ridge." Hadn't my bridegroom said, "I know you can do it, Babe"? Hadn't he grinned and hugged me and declared I could do anything I had a mind to do?

Within hours after we returned from our honeymoon—a honeymoon that had taken us to a Utah ski lodge where my husband had enrolled me in ski school with preschoolers who came only up to my quaking knees—I called a friend. "I *want* to ski," I said. Yes, I'd had a couple of stress-filled lessons, briefly considered divorce, made it off the indifferent slopes only because my spouse had held my hand and coached me all the way down. "I'm *going* to pull this off, no matter what!" I exclaimed.

My friend suggested a second ski school.

I shook my head. She couldn't see me over the phone, of course, but I knew that she knew I'd dug my heels in. "I don't have the time," I said. "I just want you to come with me."

And so she agreed to ski with me days when she didn't have to work; when she couldn't be there, I skied alone or joined other women who had it in them to be patient. I also skied with my happy spouse. "You're doin' great, Babe," he'd say, and then he'd sweet-talk me to one of the higher chairs, brag again that I could do *anything*. He even enrolled me one day in a race without breathing a single word about it to me.

"What is that on the hill?" I asked, while we were having lunch on the lodge deck.

"Slalom," he said.

"Slalom?" I shrugged. "What's a slalom?"

"A race, Babe. They're going to hold it after lunch." Grinning, he handed me an apple.

"Who's going to race?"

"Couples."

We were going to watch some couples race? Which couples? "I never . . ." I cut my apple in half. "Professionals?"

My husband shook his head. "No," he said, "just folks."

"*Which* folks?" He wouldn't, I couldn't, if he thought—
From his pack, Scotty handed me a red vest with a
number on it. "You'll do good," he said, grinning that
grin of his again.

And that day we raced. Actually, "made it down off
the hill" would be the more appropriate description, but
to tell the truth, I loved it. No one expected much from
me, so we "raced" slow. We laughed at ourselves and one
another; and when it was over, Scotty hugged me and
said, "Before the season's over, you're going with me all
the way to the top."

He was wrong, of course. I knew that for a fact, even
if he did not. Yes, in the beginning I'd said I would try
and that it would be something grand to aim for. But
after I'd skied nearly three-dozen days and still couldn't
ski a bunny hill looking like I knew what I was doing?

It wasn't until I'd skied 55 days and the season was
about to come to a close that Scotty mentioned "The
Ridge" again. "You ready?" he said.

Ready? "Scotty, be real!" There was no way, I'd begun
to explain—when I glanced back over my shoulder and
caught a glimpse of a patroller he used to date, a woman
who could go to the summit of the mountain any day of
any week. Swallowing the sane words, I returned my
husband's smile. "Okay," I said, feeling my feet glue
themselves to the bottoms of my boots. "I'll go." I yanked
off my ski hat and shook my hair free.

The next day, he told me he'd gotten permission to
take me, which hadn't been all that hard, of course, since
he headed up the patrol. We would go up the following
weekend, since there wasn't much time; the spring snow
had begun to resemble melting sugar. Before long, they'd
be closing the hill. If I was going to do this, it would have
to be now—or never.

We couldn't have asked for nicer weather. The sun
had filled the valley below, and the sky was the blue of

a prom dress. All the patrollers who would climb with us looked and acted as if this was going to be some kind of picnic—one that anyone could attend with their eyes closed. Anyone, that is, except me. Around us, people were asking if this was something I should be doing. We'd take our skis off at the top of the tallest lift and fling them over our shoulders; we'd bring our poles with us, too. And there would be a cable-like rope we'd hang onto. With my left hand, I'd cling to the rope for support. I'd carry my gear with my right hand, kick one foot into the craggy face of the hill, make certain I had a fastened foothold, slowly lift the other foot, kick it hard into the hill just ahead of the first, make certain again that I had a solid place to stand . . . and then repeat and repeat until we'd reached our destination.

It wasn't until the others had begun the climb that I thought to ask Scotty the question that had long been on my mind: "What about this 'Ridge'?" Was it narrow? Did a mountain just go up on both sides and then meet in a sort of point at the top?

Scotty laughed. "No, Babe," he said, "there's plenty of room."

"For what?" I asked. *For whom?* I squinted with my hand above my eyes. "It doesn't look like—"

Scotty stopped and squeezed my hand while the others lined up behind me.

"Okay, I can do this," I said—and pretty soon I was actually setting one foot into the ice and snow, making certain I could keep my balance, standing myself upright, and barely inching forward.

Not until we'd gotten to the top did I consider revoking every promise I'd ever made to my spouse about "until death do us part."

"The Ridge" is a ridge, plain and simple. Wide enough for a pair of skis and a little beyond—but not much. There's no highway up there and *no place* for someone who's spent most of her life with her nose in a book, stretched out on beach sand, soaking up the sun, and dreaming dreams of Tahiti and the seas in all points south.

"I can't *believe* you!" I hissed, gritting my teeth to keep myself from screaming.

"You'll do good, Babe," Scotty said, shoving off, heading south to where we would begin our descent and just as one of the best friends a novice could have said she'd be glad to ski down with me.

If it hadn't been for Jean, I'm certain I'd have lost it. As it was, I seriously considered sitting there until they sent a helicopter in for me. Otherwise, what were my choices? To the west, the mountain simply dropped. Take that route, and you had nowhere to go but the bottom. And east? Four feet of crystal-like fresh powder— and a husband who was declaring that this was going to be something I'd never forget! We were going to glide, dip, and float.

Scotty laughed and gave me another hug; he said he'd stay with me, and so would Jean.

And they did stay, and I did ski. Not like the patrollers who'd bounded off the top with their rooster tails creating sprays and rainbows. Not like my husband's old girlfriends or his current pals. I skied like those preschoolers who'd joined me for classes in the Utah ski school; but I skied. Mostly *across* the mountain to avoid skiing straight down, and sometimes I "skied" sitting down. I couldn't help it; I was scared.

When we arrived at the bottom, no one seemed to care that I hadn't exactly skied with style and grace, because they were telling me they couldn't believe I'd had "the guts." They couldn't believe I'd actually gone to the top with only one ski season under my belt. Some said they couldn't believe my husband had *let* me! (If I

remember correctly, I was the one who said that!) But
I had gone, and I'd made it, and inside I felt good.

And God? I think it's possible he also felt good about
me. I think he's always happy with us, in fact, when we
try. He's not waiting for us to do it all with dash and
class. He knows some things are difficult. He knows
there are places we don't want to go and things we don't
want to do. He knows there are obstacles and limita-
tions and personal histories that trip us up.

But he loves us . . . each and every one of us. Loves
us enough to ask us to believe that he is there and that
he's watching. He longs to have us aim for the top, to
kick a foot into the sheer fear of a thing, to hang onto
the rope, to believe that if we come off looking just a little bit clumsy and maybe even afraid, he'll nevertheless
applaud and say, "Well done."

He wants us to learn he is the God we can trust.

9

No Fish!

But they all alike began to make excuses.

Luke 14:18a

My ten-year-old had decided she wanted to fish. She'd started making her plans in the early morning. "I want to go fishing today," she said. It didn't matter that the gray of the sky hadn't yet been touched by the sun; it didn't matter that we weren't prepared, had no foods for a picnic, hadn't even located our sleeping bags for an overnight in the truck. It also didn't matter that my husband had said more than once that it was going to snow.

"It's July!" she declared, as if the adults in the family hadn't noticed. "It doesn't snow in *July*." She shook her head at the two of us and rolled her pretty eyes.

But it did snow in July in Montana. In fact, you could count on snow every month of every year. But for this child who'd been born on the West Coast, snow was the excuse the adults were making for not taking her to the river.

I suppose if it had been a more serious issue—and if she'd been naughty about it—we'd have simply put a foot down and said, "No." But she was just a little girl, and she only wanted to sleep overnight in the camper shell—and fish.

"Well, okay," Scotty said, coming out from under the truck he'd been repairing. "You let me finish up here, and then I'll find the sleeping bags and the camp stove— while you and your mom go pick out some grub."

So, on the heels of a child shouting "Hooray!" I headed into the house for my coupons, my list, and my purse. "Camping?" I breathed, raising my hand above my eyes to look at the mountains south of town. I'd grown up on the West Coast, too, but even I could see a storm brewing beyond us. Still, if Scotty had said, "Yes"?

At the supermarket, we bought marshmallows and hot dogs and pop. We stocked up on potato chips and cookies, too—just in case we wanted to stay a whole week. The "whole week" was Lisa's idea; mine was to make this a very quick trip. I didn't like the looks of the weather, nor did I think Scotty'd been making an excuse. Snow was a definite possibility—even if there was no explaining that to a child.

We hadn't driven halfway to the river when the clouds went from gray to ebony. "Snow," Scotty said, steering the pickup around the ruts an earlier storm had created. He nodded, and so did I—while, in the backseat, Lisa sat with her arms folded across her chest. It wasn't going to snow, and she wasn't going to listen to any more talk about it.

At the river, Scotty had just begun to set up the stove for cooking while Lisa and I had started laying out our bags in the back of the truck, when the first flake fell.

Followed by another . . . followed by a wind and chill that instantly reddened every nose.

"He tried to tell you," I said, shaking my head slowly at my daughter.

"Nope," she declared. She wasn't going home; the snow was going to stop pretty soon; then she and Scotty could fish.

It wasn't long before Scotty had set up the stove, but he'd also covered it with a lean-to made of tarp. By now, the wind-driven snow had begun to bite into his skin, and he almost couldn't stand up. He'd get into the back of the truck with us for a while though, he said, and maybe Lisa was right. Maybe it *would* let up.

But it didn't. In fact, that night it snowed nonstop, and the following morning you couldn't tell where the land was field and where it suddenly turned into a beaten-up road. We'd slept well, though. In fact, the weather had been conducive for some excellent sleeping. We'd also slept with our appetites satisfied, thanks to my charitable spouse. While Lisa and I had hovered in the truck under sleeping bags and blankets, he'd boiled hot dogs and chicken soup. After we'd eaten in the shelter of the camper shell, he'd also taken care of all the cleanup. But now it was morning, and the snow hadn't yet stopped—"And we *are* going home," I said.

I might as well have been talking to a stone. Seated in the cab of the truck where we had the heater running, Lisa had pulled on her striped hat and mittens, tucked her collar up around her neck, and stretched to where she could at least look tall—and as rooted as an ancient rock.

I'd just opened my mouth to say something else about our going, when I heard Scotty speak, instead. "Well, then," he was saying, "we'll just get you fixed up."

Fixed up? He was going to give in to this child? He'd opened his door, shut it quickly so as not to surround us by the cold, and headed for the back of the truck. Within seconds, he'd returned with Lisa's fishing reel and rod. "I'll just put your lure on," he said, "and then you go ahead and fish." Fish? You almost couldn't see the river for the snow! What if she got lost? What if she didn't—and fell into that freezing thing?

"Alone?" I heard Lisa peep.

Scotty nodded.

"Scotty," I said, "maybe we should—"

Scotty shook his head. "She'll be fine," he said.

I considered telling him that's why women with children shouldn't even *consider* marrying a bachelor! I considered telling him to take us all straight home—but he was grinning, and he'd winked at me, and now he was reaching over to open the passenger door for my child.

And Lisa took the bait. She grabbed her rod with the reel now attached, slid down from the bench seat to the snowy ground—and began to march.

From time to time, she'd glance back over her shoulder—and move forward several steps again. Each time she'd look back, Scotty would smile and nod. It was his way of telling her, "Keep going"—but she was going too far, and so was he. Before long she'd be there without us, and she didn't have a clue how to cast her line, let alone how to keep from casting herself in as well.

"Scotty," I said, "she can't go alone; you have to go with her." Had he lost his mind? It must have been that snow whipping him around while he'd stood outside cooking our soup.

Scotty patted my hand. "She'll be fine," he said. "You'll see."

I'd only just snapped my head back around to look out through the space Scotty had cleared across the window, when I saw my daughter disappear. Down over a knoll, the last one to cross before she'd make the river.

"That does it!" I shrilled, gripping my own door with one hand and zipping my jacket higher. "I'm going," I'd started to say—when I spotted the floppy ball of wool on the top of Lisa's knit hat. She'd only just disappeared two seconds ago, but now she was bobbing back over the hill toward the truck, making her steps long and leaning into the wind. She was coming back without our having to tell her. She'd finally understood Scotty was right and that he hadn't been trying to fool her. She was going to say, "You were right, and I'm really sorry." She was going to admit she was wrong.

I smiled as my daughter came around to the passenger side of the truck. I opened the door ready to reach out my hand to pull her up—when I heard from the little girl face that had turned both red and blue, "We might as well go home! The fish aren't biting today!"

Today when we recall Lisa's fishing story, we laugh. But when I find I'm behaving exactly the same, I remind myself that it isn't that there are "no fish." Often it's simply that something akin to stubbornness and pride has surfaced—and needs to be dealt with in me.

Part 2

When, Lord?

In the morning, O LORD, you hear my voice; in the morning I lay my requests before you and wait in expectation.

Psalm 5:3

10

Whoosh!

The LORD is near to all who call on him, to all who call
on him in truth. He fulfills the desires of those who fear
him; he hears their cry and saves them.

Psalm 145:18–19

There are those who believe God doesn't answer what
they call nonsense prayers, the prayers regarding some
"imagined" enemy—prayers that would be a "bother" to
him when he has more major matters on his mind. But
that has not been my experience with God; I see him as
the loving Father many of us longed for but never knew;
I see him as the God I can go to with absolutely anything. I can tell him my heart's desires and trust that
none of what I take to him is a nuisance, a bother, non-
sensical.

I can't truthfully say I believed these things early on
in my walk, but over the years—as I've experienced his
touch when my world seemed to have given me up—I've

heard his voice, felt his touch, watched while he worked what, for me, was a miracle. One of those miracles happened in New Mexico, only three years into my marriage and on a day when I'd learned little or nothing about entertaining a husband's boss or colleagues. In those days, we lived with cat hairs, dog hairs, chocolate brown carpet that showed not only all of those hairs but the dust and the crumbs and the spills. It was on one of those days that Scotty called me midafternoon to say he'd be bringing home out-of-town associates *and* the local boss.

"You can't be serious!" I whooped. "The house is a *mess!*" He couldn't be thinking clearly; I had nothing ready to cook, nothing to wear. "And the *carpet!*" I said, trying not to let my heavy breathing become bursts of airy panic. "I *can't* entertain," I said.

"Babe . . ." Scotty wasn't insisting, but I could hear in his voice that he needed me to do this for him, and I wanted to do this—for him.

"But . . ." I pictured the smile my husband would bring home along with his friends. I imagined how proud he would be to show off our home, even though he hadn't yet figured out that our new home was not only small but needed even more attention than we'd been able to come up with. "Okay," I said. I could do this. There weren't many hours, and I hadn't shopped for days, ironed anything, or washed my hair—but I'd be ready, I said.

As soon as we'd hung up, I started the race. First to the store and then from room to room. I would put "Moonlight Sonata" on the stereo and select some gorgeous piano music for a dinner background, though nothing was going to really make up for the way the house looked. Still, I'd pick up and dust. After that, I'd dance in the shower on first one foot and then the other. I'd make myself presentable if it was the *last* thing I did.

I'd have the house as clean as possible, too, and I'd bake a hot dish and toss a salad. I'd also toss out the dog and cat! Our teen who spilled books and clothing and cola cans from one end of the house to the other would be a different matter. But this would work.

Finally, the house nearly ready, my head wet, and Scotty's robe wrapped around me twice, I found our prettiest dishes and even one for baking that would look lovely on the table, too. I cut flowers from the backyard, polished every piece of wood in the house—except in our daughter's room. I ignored the dog with his nose pressed against the glass and the cat who'd perched himself up where he could greet the birds at my window feeder. I had no time for anything but dinner, the house, and me.

It took nearly three hours to put the dinner, the house, and me almost together. I was down to needing to change from Scotty's old robe to my clothes. I also would have to vacuum. It wasn't some obsession of mine; the carpet needed replacing, but there was no money for such things. I had no choice but to settle for running the vacuum over the cookie crumbs, cat hairs, dog hairs, and whatever else it was that made the disgusting thing look even worse. "Then I'll dress, and hooray!" I sang. Dinner was beginning to smell delicious; the cat hadn't caught a single bird; the dog had given up his post at the door for a cooler spot under the picnic table.

Jerking the vacuum out of the front hall closet, I tucked my adopted robe around me. Our canister cleaner wasn't the most wonderful machine a person could buy, but it was the one we could afford, and it had never once let me down—although we'd worked it harder than the warranty said we ought to.

Rounding the corner from the closet, I grabbed the thinning cord, plugged in the plug, flipped the switch, started pushing the brushes back and forth over what looked like sewing threads and cupcake crumbs—when I heard a murmur, a sputter, a cough, and suddenly nothing at all.

"No!" I cried. It couldn't die now, not with dinner guests only minutes from our door and me in Scotty's robe.

On my knees, I shook the hose and shook it again, but nothing happened. I grabbed it around what felt like its throat and threatened. I squeezed the plug, pulled it out, gave it a pinch, snapped it back into the wall. I flipped the switch, flipped it a second time and a third. That close to the floor, I could see the crumbs and the hairs in a way I'd never seen them before. They were a reflection not only on me and this house but on my hardworking spouse. I again checked the clock; in exactly sixteen minutes, they'd be coming. "Please," I said, shaking the entire machine by now and grabbing a fork from the table. Maybe, just maybe, there were things stuck up inside not too far, and I'd just fish them out.

But there weren't things—at least nothing there that I could see.

Jerking that hose up off the floor again, I began to shake it like a dog with a ragged slipper, and I shouted that if it didn't work I was taking it to the dump! I glanced at the clock. In exactly fifteen minutes, I could expect my husband. He'd walk through that front door expecting a fabulous meal and ready to show off his house—and his wife—but I'd be in this ugly bathrobe with my hair in sweaty ringlets around my face and with the carpet a complete disaster.

I flipped the switch back and forth, pulled the plug again, jammed it into the wall and grabbed the hose . . . and then suddenly on my knees and without thinking clearly and smelling dinner and remembering that one of the dishes *had* to be checked—I threw my hands into the air and shouted, "Can't you *help?*"—and with my words ringing in my own ears, I heard something I hadn't expected. Not the still, small voice and no singing. No angel's wings or God's voice speaking as he once spoke with Moses. Instead, I heard, "Whoosh!" Whoosh! as the hairs or the crumbs or whatever rushed up through the hose to the bag. Whoosh! as with goose bumps on my arms and legs and feeling as if I walked barefoot on hallowed ground, I completed the job I'd begun and turned our carpet into something almost lovely. Then with only minutes to spare, I checked the hot dishes, changed from Scotty's robe to something a little more becoming—and greeted my husband's smile with one of my own at the door.

Several seconds later, I was meeting Scotty's colleagues and boss, offering them a cold drink, serving them from a table with fresh-cut flowers and a dog lying quiet beside me—because God had answered my prayer. It hadn't been a prayer full of thees and thous, and my attitude hadn't been exactly right. I'd simply prayed in a tight spot, prayed a prayer that burst forth out of an urgent need. And God had heard.

Today, that's how I go to my heavenly Father. Sometimes on my knees, sometimes in the check-out lane at the supermarket. Often in a rush in the car on my way to somewhere I don't want to be or doing a chore I think I cannot handle. I just lift my heart, my thoughts, my voice to the God who loves us. It's as simple as that, and his answers come simply—even though they sometimes take time—because the God who loved us then loves us still. He desires that we come to him no matter what it is that we believe we need.

He loves us. Both me *and* you. Nothing is too difficult for him—or too small. None of our prayers, our pleas, or our fears are nonsense to God. Everything that matters to us also matters to our Creator.

It's a simple truth I've learned as I've walked through one "experience" after another: He's near to *all* who call on him. He hears not just my cries but yours. He hears because he is our heavenly Father who created us to be just a little lower than the angels. Low enough to call out to him on our knees for help—even when the "enemy" is only a vacuum cleaner.

11

One Lone Fish

"I am coming soon. Hold on to what you have, so that
no one will take your crown."

Revelation 3:11

We'd fished for days in the Colorado mountains and
caught nothing. The lake was absolutely beautiful, and
I knew I was one lucky woman. My husband planned
all the meals on our campout; he also diced red potatoes and onion and cooked my breakfast with thick-
sliced bacon over an open, wood fire—while I drank his
wonderful wake-me-up coffee. But I also wanted fish.
Fish caught by me, record-setting fish, fish to write
home about.

"What are you using for bait?" I'd been asking all the
other fishermen. They'd tell me; I'd tell Scotty; we'd
secure our campsite and drive back to the closest town.
"I need a couple of Panther Martins," I'd tell a clerk, or
maybe I'd buy a carton full of nightcrawlers, a bottle of

pink and orange eggs, or a package of miniature marsh-mallows—whatever the luckier fishermen had been using. Today would be our fourth fruitless day, though, and we'd made exactly four trips into town. The local tackle shop owner was becoming a friend of ours. Scotty thought it was cause for laughter; I did not.

"Relax, Babe," he said. "That *is* what we're here for, you know."

"Relax?" He had to be kidding. "I'm going to catch a trout, if it's the last thing I do!"

That afternoon, Scotty decided we should try fishing from the bank again, and we would fish together—but with space between us. He didn't say why, but I figured he was getting tired of watching a grown woman pout—which was fine with me. Maybe he was bringing me bad luck anyway. For sure, he didn't have his heart and mind in this enough to convince me fishing was really his sport.

We'd been fishing for about two hours. At least half-a-dozen fishermen had made their way past me on what had become a narrow stretch of ground. "What are you using?" I'd ask them, of course, and again they'd tell me and hold up a string of trout dangling from a chunk of chain or rope.

I'd just begun to tell two men they surely had a great-looking bunch of fish—when something hit my line and, in the crystal-clear water, I caught a glimpse of an enor-mous trout! Maybe the biggest fish I'd ever caught! He was sleek and gorgeous, all that I'd been dreaming of, all that I'd wished for and fished for—and now I was reeling him in and snapping my wrist sideways to land him on the one-foot width of solid ground—when he reeled and snapped, too, and then he was going side-ways toward the water. Somehow, he'd extricated him-self from my hook, and before me passed the pictures of all the frigid mornings and me with my frozen fingers gripping my rod and reel and spending all that money.

"No!" I shouted, suddenly on my knees and trumpeting at the top of my lungs. Then, with fishermen dropping their rods to watch, I grabbed that trout around his rainbow belly.

"No!" I howled again as my husband dropped his rod and headed toward where I'd been standing . . . and the water began to feel so cold . . . and I looked down and discovered I was on my knees *in* the lake—and squeezing the fish so tight I could no longer feel my fingers.

A couple of the other plaid-shirted fishermen were laughing, but I didn't care. I had my fish, and I hadn't paid him off with a wooly bugger or a Panther Martin; I hadn't fed him my nightcrawlers or any of my marshmallows in pink or green. I'd simply caught him by sheer determination, by an act of my own will.

Sometimes I wonder if this is the way God wants us to take more serious matters into our own hands. Yes, he leads us—every one of us, actually, if we'll only listen. But is it possible we have not because we give up too quickly? Because we don't persevere—or we fail to take, by the belly, those things we just plain need? And maybe even because we spend far too little time in the winter waters . . . on our knees?

12

Always Watchful, Always There

For the LORD will not reject his people; he will never forsake his inheritance.

Psalm 94:14

It isn't a topic we really want to discuss. How many times have I heard: "It isn't something a 'real Christian' considers"? We can say, "I was feeling so down" or "I had these thoughts" or "I was about to go over the wall." We can also tell ourselves and others, "I was in this mood, just exhausted, that's all." We don't say *suicide*. We don't tell anyone, not even our closest friends, what we are or were considering. We never say—even though we believe in the Lord and his goodness—we were thinking about, pondering, entertaining such an act. But why? Even Elijah "came to a broom tree, sat down under it and prayed that he might die. 'I have had enough, LORD,' he said.

'Take my life'" (1 Kings 19:4). But we're not like Elijah; we play word and head games; we hide the truth; we fear not only what man might think but what God might do with us if he knew.

But God does know; he misses nothing. He's watching every minute of every day of our years—*and* he understands. Understands life is hard, understands that sometime, somewhere—because things in our lives have wearied us on the inside—that we might consider, might entertain harmful thoughts.

I know this because I have pondered the thoughts, have put myself in a place where I might do what I felt I needed to do. I have considered taking my own life, putting an end to my feelings and fears. I have desired to bring to closure the frustration, to turn off the words in my head that said, "You never should have been born. You were just born to cause trouble. You're nothing but a disappointment to everyone."

I know this because one day—as a soon-to-be single mom—I checked into a room in a hotel far from home, sat beside the bed, stared out a dirty window—and prayed God would not only forgive me but help me take every pill in the bottle I held in the palm of my hand. My husband was making marriage preparations. I'd be divorcing in just one week, and no one had ever divorced in our family. I'd caused pain for people I hadn't wanted to hurt, including my own children. I'd seen one counselor, but all she could tell me was that I'd had a breakdown. Now, feeling I'd come to a dead end, I saw no sound way out. I had no friend from whom I could expect wise counsel, no safe place, certainly no one in the church I attended who would understand.

The morning sky had filled the room as I'd opened the drapes. It seemed the perfect beginning of a brand-new day. There would be sunshine and green growing things—but I was alone. I hadn't been a "good Christian." I hadn't prayed enough, hadn't walked in faith believing God could work *all* things for my good.

"Father," I said, "I'm so sorry." But sorry wasn't enough, was it? Wasn't that what I'd been told over and over again, not just in my home but from the pulpit? Hadn't the church women I'd worked with turned their backs? Hadn't one even said, "And here I thought you were such a good mother and wife"? Hadn't the pastor's spouse suggested I might learn to play the guitar and then I'd get the peace I needed? Only the peace hadn't come, and then her husband—when I'd asked him for wisdom—had suggested readings that weren't Christian at *all*. No, I told the Lord, I couldn't deal with this despair alone. The one woman I thought I could talk to had sent a note via her own husband, a note to tell me she didn't want to talk because I had let her down, and she was "terribly disappointed."

Picking up the bottle of pills, I turned it over and over in my hand. The sky had filled not only with blue sky and sunshine but with shades of peach and copper. The drapes were dingy, the noise beyond the door clear evidence that people were preparing to check out. And so would I. I'd take the pills, every pill. No one would care. My absence wouldn't leave much of a void.

I'd only just reached for the glass of water when I spotted a Bible on the desk beside me. "Presented by The Gideons," I read, and in the table of contents there were lists of troubles. Fear, loneliness, desperation, sin. I began to turn first one page and then another—reading words about keeping on, about trusting, about believing God was with and for me. I also read words that said when I was tempted, the Holy Spirit would come along beside me.

It isn't important that I go into all of these words, to record what was written, to say anything more than the fact that I hadn't read for more than half-an-hour when

I went to my knees, begged for strength, put the bottle away, said I'd at least try, repacked my bag, and boarded a flight back to a place that would soon no longer be my home. I wasn't certain I could do this, but I would try. I was even less certain God really was going to be there for me. After all, I'd become the perfect example of the wife and mother who'd failed. Three years later, however, God showed me how very much he had cared . . . how he had been watching . . . how he had kept me from taking the pills that would have ended a life he'd be using.

I was teaching in a Christian school in Albuquerque, and one morning one of my students came to my desk with a gift of a plaque, a plaque I still keep in plain view in my home office. He had carved it in a class, creating the dove symbol of the Holy Spirit on it, and he wanted me to have it. "I made it for you," he said. He wanted me to put it up on my wall to remember, and I was grateful. But the following week I would be even more grateful than I'd felt that morning with that beautiful plaque in my special student's hand.

"I'd like to meet you," the woman said. "My son has talked so much about you; you're his favorite teacher. In fact, I'm hearing wonderful things about your teaching."

I knew she was wrong; I hadn't done anything wonderful at all. I simply loved the kids, loved being in the same classroom with them, loved seeing them smile when they'd been told they'd "done good."

"Can you get away long enough to have soup and a sandwich?" she was asking. "Maybe someplace close to the school?"

I didn't think so; I normally graded papers during my lunch break.

"I'd really appreciate it so much," she said then. "I promise I won't take up much of your time." She just felt we should meet, felt as if she knew me, felt as if I'd already become a friend.

So I said yes. I'd meet her the following day, but I couldn't stay long. However, as I hung up, I felt a sense of something special, something in my spirit, something stirring me to the point where there were goose bumps and expectations. Not until lunch the following day did I discover why.

"You're very close to the Lord," the mother said. "Right?"

I nodded.

"Me, too." She smiled. "I think that's just one of the reasons I've felt connected to you," she added. "But where have you come from? Are you a local, or did you move from somewhere to here?"

I told her I'd moved; my new husband's work had relocated us just one year ago.

"And where before that?" she wanted to know.

She was getting so close; I was beginning to wish lunch would come to an end and I could return to my room with my books and my coffee and a red pen. I didn't choose to go into my life history; I'd been blessed with a new beginning. I wanted to turn the conversation around; I was telling her far too much—"So what about you?" I asked. Where was she from? We should be talking about *her*.

"We moved here from," she began . . . but suddenly the room grew small and warm. She'd named *the* state, *the* city . . . the place with the Gideon Bible.

My ears ringing, I began to gather my purse. Not since the morning I'd picked up the pills had I thought about this state too many miles away from home.

"I worked with The Gideons," she said.

The chill began on the bottoms of my feet and began to wrap itself around me. "You worked with—?"

"Auxiliary," she said. "But have you ever been to—?"

My throat felt as if it had closed, and I nodded. But then—before I could stop myself—I began to tell her everything. "But a Gideon Bible . . ." I said, trying without success to stop the tears. "I picked it up . . ." I was telling her too much; this woman couldn't possibly understand; she'd be asking the headmaster to remove her son from my class and then—

But she wasn't leaving. Instead, she began to fight tears, too. "Nancy," she said, leaning forward in her chair. "Nancy . . ." She slowly picked a napkin up off the table and began to wipe her eyes. "Do you know what the auxiliary does . . . did?" She looked straight at me and again put her napkin down. "We place Bibles in hotels," she said. "And . . . and . . ." She paused as the room seemed to grow not only small but quiet. "And that was *my* hotel to cover; *I* placed that Bible in your room."

The Bible, God's grace, and his forgiveness had come full circle. He'd been watching then; he was watching still. "I will never leave you nor forsake you," he'd said in his own Word. "Never" meant just that, not ever. Not when I'd been a disappointment to myself and to the others. Not when I'd caused pain or felt abandoned by the people I'd been so very close to. "Never," he'd said, and at that table with the mother of the boy who'd given the gift, I was given another . . . a reminder that when you and I can't walk on water, he is *always* watchful, *always* there.

13

There's No Such Thing as a Free Lunch?

In his heart a man plans his course, but the LORD determines his steps.

Proverbs 16:9

It wasn't like my husband to stand me up, but I'd waited for over an hour, and the lunch crowd had all gone back to work . . . and still I sat alone . . . impatiently waiting.

It also wasn't like him not to call. My husband's a considerate man. He bends over backwards for people—especially me. But he'd invited me to meet him for lunch, and now I'd sat in this café feeling awkward and telling the waitress countless times, "Not yet, but my husband *is* coming."

I don't brag about my short fuse; most days I work hard not to even own it. But it's there all the same, ready for whatever might come along to set me off—and that day in Albuquerque, with the best green chili in town coming out of that incredible kitchen and with me dressed up—and after driving in heavy traffic from all the way north to downtown? I blew up. Not out loud, mind you. I'm quite adept at holding back when necessary. No, I detonated in silence. Thanked the waitress for the several glasses of water, told her my husband really never did anything like this, said if he came in later—because they all knew him—to say that I'd gone home. "No," I told her, I didn't want to call him. Actually, I didn't have a number to call; at this particular point in his career, he didn't have one of his own and, though I didn't say so, I had no way to reach him.

Back in traffic, having "calmly" made my exit, I listed for myself all the ways I would tell him just how *furious* I'd been. There was no excuse I could think of for embarrassing a wife. Surely, he couldn't have forgotten. We'd talked that very morning about how we looked forward to these times together; he'd said my coming into town made his day.

"Some *day*," I spewed, wheeling around one vehicle and then another. If he thought I was *ever* again going to drop everything and drive into town for him. "Hah!" I whooped, glaring at a driver driving beside me. Let him find someone *else* to meet him for lunch. Let *him* just sit there and see how it feels to be stood up. Let *him* go without lunch—and, no, I wouldn't cry. If the man had no manners, then it was time I found this out. Even though we'd been married for going on four years, I evidently had a whole lot more to learn—and so did he, I told myself. And tonight when he got home? I was going to give him an earful!

My pulse racing and feeling a shortness of breath— even though I was *driving* uphill and not running—I'd just entered an intersection when, without one single thought in my head about it, I turned left. *Left?* I frowned at myself in the mirror. My house wasn't left; I had several more blocks to go before I should have turned anywhere. But I had turned. Not only that, I had a keen sense of the direction I was going and an even keener sense regarding my destination.

In front of a school—with my engine still running and my adrenalin pumping even harder—I looked to see where the entrance was and turned my wheels into the parking lot. I'd never been here before, but I was going to go inside and introduce myself. *I'll tell them I'm not currently teaching, but . . .*

"You're looking for a teaching job?" A secretary eating a sandwich at the front desk turned to the woman eating at a table in the back. "I'm sorry," she said, "it's midyear . . . and . . . we have all the teachers we need."

I shook my head, looked directly at her, caught the Christian high school's logo out of the corner of my eye. "I'll just fill out an application *or* talk to someone," I said.

"Someone?"

I nodded and mentally dug my heels in. "Your principal?"

"We have a headmaster." Her shoulders raised, the secretary drew a deep breath. She'd been working and trying to eat, but I'd interrupted, and she was probably thinking, *This woman's a certified nut.*

"I'll talk to him then," I said, all the while telling myself I'd lost it completely now. I knew no one here, knew almost nothing about the school, had agreed not to teach while we settled into our most recent relocation and helped our daughter adjust.

"Our headmaster isn't here," the secretary said.

"I'll wait." I'd wait? I glanced at the second woman; she thought I was some kind of crackpot as well. And why not? I'd never done anything like this before. It was my husband's fault; he'd made me so mad!

"He won't be coming back today," the woman said. She tried a smile. "But if you'd like to call next week."

"I'd like an application," I said.

If you're as old as I am, then maybe you remember a black-and-white television program called *The Buster Brown Show*. On it there was this creature who'd pop up out of a box or something. He'd trick people into saying words they didn't mean to say. His name was Froggy the Gremlin. Standing at that desk that day, I felt as if Froggy had hidden somewhere behind me and was giving me all the wrong words—when all I wanted was to flee, to go home, to forget I'd ever been this pushy.

The woman was handing me an official-looking form. "If you'd like to take this with you," she said, "we can—"

"I'll fill it out here." I'd fill it out here? I wasn't actually going to *teach*; I was just angry with my husband, acting out that anger. And what about tomorrow, when this day was behind me, and he'd said he was sorry, and I'd said, "I forgive"?

The woman's coworker had come to the front desk. Together they were watching me with puzzled faces.

"Thanks," I said, reaching for the pages of paper. "I'd prefer to fill it out here, if you don't mind."

"I don't mind," the first secretary said, "but as you can see, we haven't much space—"

"I'll sit out in the hallway," I said, fishing a pen from my purse and turning toward a student desk up against a wall next to stacks of boxes.

Within seconds, I'd begun to record all the places I'd lived and taught. I noted that I'd graduated college at an age when most of the women I knew were doing other things . . . leading groups of Girl Scouts and directing choirs at some church. I wrote that I'd taught English in Seattle, that I'd substituted in Montana, earned all the credits for a second advanced degree. I gave them my home address and number and my husband's work address, too—but noted he had no phone. Then, dropping the application on the woman's desk—because, by now, she'd disappeared along with her friend—I headed for the main road home. I was no longer angry with my spouse; I was angry with me. I'd wasted time not only at that café but here, as well. Not only that, I'd wasted this woman's time and paper. "Ridiculous," I breathed, pulling up into my driveway. *I hope I never see them again. I hope they never see me.* I'd made a fool of myself, acted pushy; I knew nothing about the school, for heaven's sake!

That night, Scotty came home with flowers. "I'm sorry, Babe," he said. He'd been called into a meeting, a command performance, unavoidable. Once the "short" session had begun, it became clear that it was going to go on forever, and he couldn't leave the room. There was no way to tell me.

I told him I was sorry, too, that I'd gotten myself all worked up. So worked up, I told him, that I'd applied for a job.

Together, we laughed. A job? Who was going to hire some stranger who pushed her way into an office?

That was Friday. On Sunday night, the phone rang. "Nancy Hoag?" I heard a strange man's voice say.

"Yes," I said, wondering who in the world would call so late. Everyone who knew me knew I went to bed even before the kids in our neighborhood.

"You don't know me," he said. "But I'm the headmaster at the Christian high school."

I sat down. The headmaster? He wanted to tell me he didn't ever want me to set foot again in his school?

"This is a strange one," he was saying now. "But . . ." The man cleared his throat. "Well, over the weekend . . . our English teacher has had what the doctors are calling a 'breakdown'." He cleared his throat again. "She won't be back . . . and we were wondering . . ."

Scotty had come to stand by my chair.

"Yes?" I said, thinking I should say something more, but waiting because I couldn't find the words I needed.

"Wondering," he said, "if you could come in tomorrow morning. We're going to need someone to finish up the year."

They were going to need someone? I hadn't just pushed my way in? I'd been led? God had worked the broken lunch date for good? Was it possible he'd been working all along to get me to the place where I would go to that school and apply?

"Yes," I said, nodding for my puzzled husband. "I'll be happy to teach English to your students." This time, I smiled and received Scotty's smile in return.

For the rest of that year and all of the next, I taught, helped lead chapel, painted classroom walls, directed a choir, and monitored the lunchroom. Not always with a keen sense of liking what I was doing, but with the very real awareness that I'd been called. There were days when I longed to be home, days when I longed to meet my husband for lunch or when my daughter's school needed parent volunteers, and I wanted one of those parents to be me. "That's my prayer," I told several of my fellow teachers, nearing the end of my second year— and one day a man came to our secretary's office. He'd just retired and was looking to teach again, but this time in a Christian school. His specialty was English, he wanted the work—and I was ready. It was time for me to go home.

For the school, for this man, for me . . . God was again working *all* things for good.

He was also teaching me—had been teaching me from the day my husband had missed our lunch date—to see how he guides me by his own hand.

14

The Release Cut

"He cuts off every branch in me that bears no fruit, while every branch that does bear fruit he prunes so that it will be even more fruitful."

John 15:2

The clock in my kitchen might have said otherwise, but my day had been longer than most. I wanted nightfall to come; I wanted to collapse into bed; once there, I'd pull the pillow over my head and dream of never getting up again. Not twelve hours earlier—when I'd crawled out from under those same covers, reluctantly shoved cold feet into fleece boots, and plodded to the kitchen so dark I almost couldn't find the light, I'd wallowed in an identical mood.

Our finances weren't the worst I'd ever heard of, but for several months we had struggled. We'd made an expensive trek to the Northwest for what we'd hoped would be a family reunion, but it hadn't been what I'd dreamed about at all. Now we had returned to our Southwest town short on both finances and joy. For weeks, I'd reflected, prayed, and asked, "Why?" Why, on the heels of the costly reunion, had our household expenses increased? Why had the school system let teachers go? Why had I lost my teaching job? And what about my older children? One on the West Coast, the other back east? How long would it take me to save for airfares now? When would I see them again? I hadn't even had money enough to celebrate their college accomplishments—and I'd begun to blame God. "You've allowed too much trimming this time," I said.

Meanwhile, my youngest was a good girl and helpful, but in just one week, I'd had at least two "discussions" with her. She had decided that her friends—also in their early teens—had more of everything material while she had "none of the above." She couldn't understand that I hadn't been making up excuses; we really were in no position to buy the extras she "just had to have." With my fears looming large regarding our income and our child, my spirit had become more than a little heavy. Nevertheless, it was time for supper; I had a table to set and foods to prepare. Even if I wanted quiet and space alone, I wasn't going to have it. That became even more obvious when Lisa suddenly danced across the kitchen and slid into her chair. "Mom! I have to have one! Please?" she chirped without taking a breath. "A 'release cut' I mean," she said.

"A what?" Was a mother with a headache actually expected to—?

"You know," Lisa groaned. She didn't say, "Mom, you never understand *anything!*" but she had that look. "A *re-lease* cut?" she said.

I gave my husband one of *my* looks. The one that said, "What in the world is she talking about?" I wanted to pull a Greta Garbo; I wanted to be left alone. Why was this child bothering me?

Pushing leftovers from one side of my plate to the other, I could hear Lisa trying to convince my husband, but all I could think about was his latest news. "Federal funding cutbacks," he'd said. Some employees would be furloughed; others would be let go. While it didn't appear that he would be discharged, the cutbacks would again affect the money he'd bring home.

"Mom, you're *not* listening!" Lisa raised her eyebrows. She was right about *that*. "Okay," I said, "I'll try."

"Mom, it's a really great cut, and I know you're going to like it."

Father, I prayed, it's so difficult for us right now. If I just understood . . .

I turned again to look directly at my daughter. "Lisa," I said, hoping I didn't sound as wretched as I felt. "Maybe you could explain *exactly* what this 'release cut' is?"

"Oh, Mom." Lisa shook her head. "Well . . . today in class, one of the models—who's also a hairdresser—demonstrated hairstyles and told me I need one," she said, beaming. "So . . . can I? She says it's going to be perfect for my curly hair, and I'll look so much better, and it'll really help me get modeling jobs."

Jobs? Modeling what? We'd given her the lessons as a birthday present, but we hadn't actually expected . . . and now there would be this additional expense? "Honey," I said, "I don't really—" I wasn't prepared for this, but how could I say no when my daughter was so excited? None of what we were walking through was her fault. "On the other hand, if it's okay with—"

My husband was grinning his father grin. "Okay with me," he said.

Okay with him? "Fine, then," I said, shrugging. But now Lisa was explaining not only that she needed to make an appointment right away but that it was going to cost "a little more than" we usually paid for such things.

"How 'little more'?" I asked.

"Fifty dollars."

"Fifty—?" I wouldn't shriek; shrieking wouldn't help. I stared at Scotty, instead.

"Lisa," Scotty started to say.

"What in the *world?*" I blurted.

"Mom, you don't get it."

No, I did not.

"It's not like other kinds of cuts, Mom. The stylist said because I have all of this natural curl—"

Curl? We almost couldn't get a brush through it.

"Well, they call it a 'release cut' because they cut your hair just the right way, and it brings out the hidden attributes." She was beaming again. "It will be *released* to become the best it can be. See, Mom? See?"

And, suddenly—with my fork in midair—I not only saw but heard. God was answering my prayers. I'd gone to him with, "Why all of these cutbacks and the pruning?"—and now he was showing me why. Just as Lisa would be thrilled with her new appearance, so would I rejoice one day when the Lord finished restyling and reshaping me.

"Yes," I said, smiling at last with my daughter. "I see." I didn't say I understood completely yet, because I did not. But that God was with us, that his reasons were good, that he knew what it was that needed cutting? That much had become clear. He would cut everything from our lives that we did not need; and one day we would bear not only more but better fruit. Because we would be released.

15

My Most Embarrassing Moment Almost

When pride comes, then comes disgrace, but with humility comes wisdom.

Proverbs 11:2

It would be recorded that I had been the first woman ever to speak from this podium. In the past, it hadn't been allowed, but female friends, all members of this dignified church, had worked very hard, and finally, their reluctant pastor—who would be out of town—had said, "Oh, okay."

Now here I stood with my smiling allies *and* my husband cheering for me. I'd spoken for nearly an hour, basked in the laughter that erupted in all the right spots, delighted in the nods and smiles. I'd said what I'd come to say and mentally patted myself on the back, noted that my words had been well-received. I didn't wish to entertain pride, but this flock was one of the largest around, and the pews were packed, and I now was beginning to make my way down from the pulpit to a sanctuary filled with applause. *Yes, this is definitely cause for rejoicing,* I was in the middle of telling myself—when all of a sudden I spotted the sound man literally running from the back of the sanctuary! Not only running but waving! Worse, he was waving at *me!* Did he not know how to behave?

I offered a feeble smile, continued to sashay in my new suit, cast a confused glance at my husband—and discovered he was also making preparations to stand. Worse, he was also looking like a man about to take off on a run!

My own husband was standing? *No! Sit down!* I started to frown, had begun to shake my head—when I heard something behind me collapse.

My friends looked shocked. The first awful racket had been followed by another thud and thump.

I shot a second glance at my spouse. Was he laughing? Beginning to cry?

I twirled to where the noise had come from—and spotted the sound man again. No longer waving but hopping, looking breathless, and moving in.

I'd scarcely stumbled to the side of the aisle in order to let him pass by me to *wherever* he thought he was going—when with one swift, masterful move he seized *my* tiny microphone, uncoupled the clip, and freed it from *my* lapel.

Stunned, I stared over the young man's shoulder and at "my" pulpit—surrounded by books, pens, and papers dumped and shuffled onto and across the plush, red-carpeted floor. I'd come away with the power cord connected.

Later that week, several of us met to discuss *my* message. "Unforgettable," some said.

But God's? Even more "impacting" than mine.

16

He Wouldn't Be
Coming Back

"For your Maker is your husband—the Lord Almighty is his name."

Isaiah 54:5a

My neighbor, Karen, and I had been commuting more miles than we'd wanted to and teaching in the same conflict-ridden school—which meant life for us, some days, could be overwhelming. For Karen, there were also things going on at home that made her days and nights even more overwhelming than mine.

"Still," she'd say, "I'm trusting God." Her marriage wasn't always what she wanted it to be, and her husband had begun making matters worse by frequently staying away from home. "One day though," she'd say, "he'll get it together; he's trying very hard."

Mornings, driving to school, we would talk. On our lunch breaks, we would pray. If she could just be more fun after work, she'd tell me, then maybe her husband would be happier with her. She'd go home and bake his favorite pie, try to keep their kids quiet, do whatever her husband wanted. She'd fit into every one of his plans; in fact, she was working outside her home because he'd asked her to. No matter how tired or fearful she felt some days, she refused to come right out and complain—until one afternoon when we'd gotten home late.

I'd dropped Karen off in her driveway and driven the three blocks to my own, when my telephone rang. "He's left me," I heard my friend sobbing. "He's left me, and he's taken all of his things. He's gone, and he took . . ."

"Karen?" I couldn't believe it, but I also wasn't surprised. "He took what?" I asked. And where was he now?

He'd cleaned out the garage and had taken all of his personal belongings and clothing. He'd left only a note; there was someone else he loved better. He'd stopped loving Karen a long time ago, and he wouldn't be coming back to her or their girls.

"Help me; you've got to help," my friend wept. "I . . . I . . . don't know what to do."

And neither did I. "But I'm coming," I said. She had put up with so much. "I'll tell my family; I'm on my way right now." But would Karen's kids be okay?

They weren't yet aware that anything had happened; this was their night for piano lessons, and a friend had picked them up.

When I pulled up into her driveway, I remember feeling afraid. Karen looked so much worse than I'd expected; she was sobbing and shaking uncontrollably.

"I'm taking you to my house," I said.

"No!" she cried. She wanted to go somewhere where no one knew her. It had started to rain; we could go to a family restaurant at the bottom of the hill. We could

89

get a booth and sit somewhere in the back; no one would even know we were there. No sooner had we pulled into the parking lot, however, when thunder and lightning began to fill the sky. We were both afraid to get out of the car. We could just sit here in the parking lot, I said—when Karen began to cry again.

"What am I going to do?" she kept repeating. She had a decent job, but she didn't make a bunch of money. "I can't make it on my own." Her children needed her at home before and after school, but she'd never be able to stay home with them again. If only she'd tried harder, figured out what it was he'd wanted.

God, please, I kept praying. What could I tell a woman about a husband I'd never met? How could I counsel or even suggest? Should she try to find him and plead with him to come home? Would he, even if she promised to be whatever?

I stared at the rain on my window and pictured Karen's two darling girls. I felt my friend's pain fill my thoughts and my throat with what I hadn't wanted to think about but what I needed to remember. I'd been there once, alone, divorced, and not knowing what to do. For me, it had been a long process—the healing, the growing—none of it had come quickly. Some days, I'd even behaved badly. Every step had been difficult. Without the Lord and the handful of helping friends who knew him and stuck by me, I never would have made it. I understood abandonment.

"I'm never going to make it," Karen said, still trying not to cry and making a clearing on the foggy glass. "I tried," she said. "I really tried."

"Yes," I said, "you did." There were times, in fact, when I had wondered why she hadn't *asked* her husband to leave—at least temporarily. He hadn't been loving; he'd been abusive. Still, as Christians, we were supposed to forgive seventy times seven. "Father . . ." I breathed.

I've done my forgiving, so please don't make me remember what I no longer need to recall. What I needed was a word for my friend; we could consider all the possibilities and details later. I would go with her to see a pastor, a counselor, anyone who could give her the wise counsel she was seeking, I said. But she was looking at me again. "Tell me what to do right *now*," she cried. "Tell me what to do."

"I can't." I couldn't. When healing came for me, it had come so completely that to recall the details, the specific steps—"The girls . . ." I heard myself say, as I caught a glimpse of my former self and the end of a day when the grief had been so heavy my nine-year-old had come to tuck me in. It was that night that I made myself see I had a child to go on for; I had a little girl who needed me to behave like her mom.

"The girls," I said again. "You might hate where you find yourself." I had. "But tomorrow—for your girls—" I said, trying to sound more clearheaded than I felt, "you have to shower, dress, prepare breakfast, and get you and your girls off to where each of you needs to go."

Karen was still looking at me.

"Because . . ." I said, feeling just a little more confident, feeling as if maybe I could at least say something that would help, "as long as you're in the water, you might as well learn to swim."

At first, Karen said nothing, as I mentally walked through the steps I'd once reluctantly taken and through the despair I'd once felt. Then, my friend nodded; her crying had stopped. What I'd said had sounded so dispassionate—even to my own ears—but Karen was wiping her eyes and gathering herself together. She needed to go pick up her girls, she said. They wouldn't yet have had their supper. "But . . . this is so hard," she breathed.

"Yes," I said, remembering having to pick up my own child and thinking surely God must have turned his head. "But your children need you to be their mother."

Straightening her hair in the rearview mirror, Karen tucked her coat collar up. There would be homework and baths to tend to and then prayers and bedtime, she said. Tomorrow—once she'd had a chance to think clearly—she'd decide just exactly what she needed to do. "But, for now," she said—still shaken but no longer weeping—"I'll swim."

17

Dressed for the Occasion

"Consider how the lilies grow. . . . If that is how God
clothes the grass of the field . . . how much more will he
clothe you, O you of little faith!"

Luke 12:27–28

The story is a long one. It began when I was seventeen,
with my marrying only weeks out of high school and
with my being unable to go to college—thus adding to
baggage I already carried regarding my insignificance.
Now, divorced for several years and remarried, and with
two of my three children deciding to live with their
father and his family, my firstborn had sent me an
announcement. She'd be participating in a beauty pageant and, to see her, my husband and I would drive two
days from an ordinary neighborhood to one we considered well-to-do. We would do so in an aging pickup
truck. Worse, my husband owned only one out-of-style
suit, and I had no idea *what* I would wear.

Scotty admitted he knew little about women's cloth-ing or pageants, but if I was worried, then we were going to buy me something brand new. "If you need or want a new outfit, Babe," he said, "then we're going to get it for you."

A real outfit? Maybe something long and elegant? Per-haps both an elegant shawl and a gown? I'd never even owned one for my own high school prom. For that occa-sion, I'd had to borrow a dress. For both my first and second weddings, I'd purchased something unbecom-ing but inexpensive—and embarrassed myself. Still, I didn't want my husband to feel as if we needed to shop. On the other hand, every time I'd say we didn't have to do this, Scotty would smile and say, "We're *going*"—which meant we were going to the mall. So, one week before my daughter's pageant, I bought myself a floor-length shimmery thing with spaghetti straps—and headed home to sew. I'd create a wrap from fabric I already owned. Fabric with a black background, pink flowers, yellow flowers, and flowers done in blue—and with leaves that perfectly matched my emerald green gown.

Modeling for my husband, I couldn't help but smile. Scotty had said I would be beautiful on the evening of our occasion. Before we packed and pulled out, he also said he would be buying me a garment bag of my own. "But we can't replace the truck," he added, giving me a hug.

During the two-day trip, I helped with the driving and checked on the dress just once. Not until we'd parked in front of our motel, did we open the back of the camper shell a second time—and not until then did I discover that, while traveling in a rainstorm, my new burgundy garment bag had been soaked. On my exquisite emer-ald-green gown were spots the size of a cup. Spots that would never be coming out.

"We'll buy you a new dress," Scotty said, wrapping me in his arms. If I'd just stop crying and get myself ready, we'd look for a shopping mall.

"No," I said, trying to act like the grown-up I was supposed to be. I couldn't let my husband spend more money. We'd prayed God would watch over us *and* this trip; if the dress was ruined, it was ruined. I wouldn't pretend to understand why; maybe I'd made too much of immaterial material; maybe God hadn't wanted us to drive out here at all. Whatever the reason, this junket had already become expensive enough. Besides, I'd done some teaching the week before last, so now I had decent street clothes I could substitute.

"Babe," Scotty began, "you had your heart set—"

"I'll wear what I have," I said.

When we pulled into the parking lot of the posh hotel, Scotty reached over and squeezed my hand. For my sake, he'd dressed in khakis and a casual shirt. "You'll be the most beautiful woman there," he said.

Beautiful? I'd never once felt beautiful; why would I feel beautiful now? "In street clothes?" I almost said aloud. I returned my husband's hand squeeze as we headed for the front doors and began to make our way through the packed and clamorous lobby. Evidently there was to be more than one function in this place, and the people who were here for something else were dressed in casual dress. Just like Scotty and me.

We'd only just turned to ask a bellhop for directions, when I suddenly realized we were here! Every one of the members of the milling crowd, moving in bunches and rapidly talking clusters, was headed for the great hall. None of them in gowns.

Catching a quick glance again at my husband, I saw that he was smiling, and I knew that if our truck shell hadn't leaked and if my dress hadn't become stained, I'd have been the only one in something shimmering with

spaghetti straps . . . the only woman in a full-length gown
. . . the only woman feeling and looking foolish. I also
knew—beyond a shadow of a doubt—that not only had
God blessed me with a generous and loving spouse, he
had given us the rainstorm—and seen to it that I was
properly dressed.

Part 3

Where, Lord?

This is what the LORD says—your Redeemer, the Holy
One of Israel: "I am the LORD your God, who teaches you
what is best for you, who directs you in the way you
should go."

Isaiah 48:17

18

Sticks and Stones

The words of the wise are like goads, their collected sayings like firmly embedded nails—given by one Shepherd.

Ecclesiastes 12:11

Several years ago, I read a letter to an editor; in it the writer said, "Most of us have met self-appointed saints who, by their abrasive approach, have driven people away from Christianity—I actually heard one such Elijah brag that his message was so strong that few could accept it." Another wrote to this same editor, however, that "Christians can't always be 'nice.'"

Well, I met a "saint" once—one I wanted to label "self-appointed." What I soon discovered, however, was a woman who couldn't always be "nice"—because she'd chosen to be truthful instead.

I met Grace in my driveway at my garage sale and, because I'd only just moved into the neighborhood, I was delighted when she introduced herself and invited me to her house for coffee. I was even more pleased when she asked, "Are you a Christian?"

"Yes!" I exclaimed.

"I knew it," she said. "I could hear it in your voice."

A perfect stranger had identified me as a believer simply because she'd heard my voice? I smiled, hoped I looked humble, felt more than a little proud. That was the last proud thought I'd have for some time.

The following week, we met in my new friend's sunny kitchen where the coffee couldn't have been better. I was beginning to feel like a curled up cat—until Grace looked me in the eye and said, "You know, back at your garage sale? I didn't just hear you were a believer, I overheard something else; you were making a joke about your husband's being 'all thumbs' when it came to dealing with some sale." She hadn't meant to listen, she added, filling my cup. "But a woman's words can *destroy* her husband."

What in the world? Surely she wasn't referring to some casual comment I'd made. How rude! The woman was clueless. I loved Scotty, and was about to say so, but now she was repeating herself.

"A woman can actually destroy her own husband," she said again.

A rebuttal on the tip of my tongue, I opened my mouth to speak, uttered something garbled, remembered my husband's closet full of the shirts I'd laundered—remembered the baking I'd begun earlier and the gardening I would tend to when I got out of here. My husband was lucky to have me, and this woman had no business—

"Nancy, are you listening?" Grace asked, focusing on me as if I were some child in her Sunday school room.

"Oh yes, that's awful," I said, pretending to hang onto the woman's every word but thinking I didn't need friends badly enough to put up with this. "You're right," I said. "I know I can certainly be hurt by words." I recalled childhood fights when one kid and then another had heckled me. "But," I said, "I'd simply shout 'Sticks and stones may break my bones, but words will never hurt me!'" There now, maybe this woman would back off.

Grace smiled, but she wasn't amused. Worse, before I could say another word, she'd opened her Bible to Proverbs 12:4 and propped it between us. "A virtuous woman is a crown to her husband: but she that maketh ashamed is as rottenness in his bones," she read.

I screwed up my mouth. I wanted to say, "You know, a person needs to *earn* the right to be heard!"—but Grace had already flipped to another passage: Proverbs 18:8.

"The words of a talebearer are as wounds, and they go down into the innermost parts of the belly." She'd practically groaned, as though the reading pained her.

I couldn't help wondering how she thought I felt. *Good grief, what a terrible hostess!* She was making me uncomfortable, and now she was reading that passage over again. This time—in place of "talebearer"—she'd substituted "wife."

What sort of coffee conversation was this?

"As a mad man who casteth firebrands, arrows, and death, So is the man [wife] that deceiveth his neighbour [her husband], and saith, Am not I in sport?" she read from Proverbs 26:18–19.

"The Scripture passage didn't say 'wife,'" I said—raising my voice. I'd had just about enough.

"Yes," Grace said, "but a truth is a truth."

A truth? As in *the* truth? "But doesn't every wife joke some?" My feet had begun to fidget beneath what was becoming an *un*-easy chair.

"Scripture seems to say it's not a joking matter." Grace didn't sound angry, but neither did she smile.

"Oh, for heaven's sake," I said. Most of us joked around—all of us but Grace. As a kid, hadn't I been praised for my sense of humor? It was a strength, wasn't it? A "quick wit," they'd called it, and at an early age I'd learned it attracted attention, and I liked that. I'd only just begun to open my mouth in my defense when, without warning, Grace was interrupting me with yet another verse: Proverbs 19:13b.

"The contentions of a wife are a continual dropping," she said.

"Okay, wait just one minute—"

"My (husband's) inmost being will rejoice when (his wife's) lips speak what is right," she added, reading Proverbs 23:16.

Okay, that had really done it. *I'm out of here,* I told myself. "I want to know where it says that," I told Grace. The woman had missed her calling; a pulpit was what she needed. I tried a second time to get to my feet and to come up with a way to flee graciously, but Grace had started flipping from one dog-eared chapter to another. She'd pause and read from two Bibles, and every word she read seemed to support *her* and not *me.*

"Do you know," she continued, "'inmost' refers to the mind, heart, *and* spirit? That's powerful when you stop to think about it."

Now I'd really had it; my new "friend" was hung up about something that had nothing whatsoever to do with me. This would teach me. No more talking to perfect strangers—and no more dropping in for coffee in this decidedly strange neighborhood.

I'd barely pushed my chair away from the table when Grace gave me a look that clearly said, "You sit down."

And I sat—and heard myself say, "Grace, do you think a man's *stress* could be related to the words that come out of his wife's mouth?"

"It's possible." Grace nodded. "In fact, I think Scripture makes a stronger statement than that."

I immediately pictured my husband and the look on his face earlier in the day when I'd told yet another "little joke" about a miscalculation he'd made. What if this woman was right? "Besides stress, what about lack of confidence and depression?" Surely Scotty understood my jokes were just in fun—didn't he?

By now, Grace had read and commented for nearly an hour. She'd never once refilled our cups, but I wasn't about to say a word about seconds. I wanted one thing and one thing only: I wanted to bring this conversation to some sort of conclusion, and then I was out of here.

"Set a watch, O LORD, before my mouth; keep the door of my lips," Grace was reading from Psalm 141:3.

Wait just one minute! Weren't we supposed to receive *comfort* from the Psalms? The woman didn't deserve politeness from me; this was the last straw. I gave a made-up excuse, gathered my belongings, and fled.

In my own kitchen, I tried to calm down, but the woman had made me angry. If I listened to a favorite radio ministry, I'd feel better.

I turned the dial to a familiar station, heard a voice I knew, and anticipated encouragement. What I heard, instead, was Grace's echo.

"It's time our tongues grew up," Karen Mains was saying. "As children we may have been laughed at or with because of the 'cute' things we'd said. But as adults, our words too often cut others deeply." The title of her topic? "The Tongue: Everybody's Problem."

Was God speaking to me through this woman? Had he been speaking to me even through Grace?

I cradled my head in the palms of my hands. "Lord, am I guilty?"

"Vilify," I heard—just as subtly but as surely as I'd heard my heart beat. *Vilify?* Had I understood the word before and simply forgotten—or had the Holy Spirit dropped it into my thoughts?

Feeling like a child on a treasure hunt, I found a dictionary in our hall closet. Within seconds, I'd located my word. "Vilify," I read. "To use openly abusive language of or about"—and I remembered an evening and my husband's despair as he'd shared his concern about his work and our financial situation. His lanky frame had slumped with discouragement. But my response? I'd joked about the poorhouse; I'd even "just happened to mention" the time he'd cut the dining room moulding four inches too short. But now—because Grace had been discerning, and Karen Mains had taught with wisdom, and God had done a thorough work—I understood my careless words had wounded my spouse *and* our relationship.

"God, forgive me," I breathed, dropping to my knees. "I've sinned against my husband and you. Please heal Scotty; take away any pain I've inflicted; bind the wounds so completely he'll remember them no more." Then I dialed my husband's office.

"Scotty, I'm sorry," I cried. "Please forgive me." I told him how much I loved him, how grateful I was for him and all that he had done for us. I promised I would try never to "make jokes" again.

As I ran out of both breath and words, I heard my husband chuckle. He was busy, he was saying, so we couldn't talk long, but he was looking forward to coming home. We could even go out for dinner if I wanted. Again, I heard his comforting laughter—which was all the confirmation I needed that his wounds were already healing.

"You can be the music in your husband's heart," Grace had said earlier that morning—and slipping the receiver into its cradle, I vowed I would be that music. With God's help, I would never speak sticks and stones again—because, like the apostle Paul, Grace had spoken the truth, and she'd done so not with sugary words but in love.

19

Lisa's Angel

For he will command his angels concerning you to guard you in all your ways. . . ."Because he loves me," says the Lord, "I will rescue him; I will protect him, for he acknowledges my name."

Psalm 91:11, 14

We'd gone to bed weary. Weary, because it was nearly 11:30 P.M. and we normally went to bed by nine; weary, because I was worried about my daughter. Only weeks out of a university in Washington State, she'd moved on her own to Washington, D.C.—closer to where my husband and I were living in Pennsylvania, but not nearly close enough for me. I never turned on the news that I didn't hear about muggings, murder, and rape. Did Lisa understand what it meant to be young and single, boarding subways at night, and living alone?

"I wish you hadn't moved there," I'd told her over the phone. Yes, her apartment was charming with colonial brick and wooden shutters and a parklike setting and creek. But tonight I was worried, and I'd been talking to my husband about it until finally he'd said he just couldn't talk any more. He'd gone to bed just minutes before me, had fallen asleep almost immediately, and now it was time for me to sleep as well. But I couldn't. Instead, I prayed.

"Father, I'm worried about Lisa," I whispered. She would be closing the store where she worked, walking alone from the mall, waiting on a poorly lit corner to ride a late-night bus, and transferring to the Metro underground. When she finally arrived at her stop, she'd cross a street hidden by vacated buildings and offices closed until the following day. From there, she'd travel three blocks down uneven, dimly lit stairs between more darkened buildings identical to her own. Some nights, she also darted through a tunnel to shorten the distance—which meant she'd be visible to no one except any strangers who might be in that tunnel, too.

"Father," I breathed again. "She trusts you; *please* take care of her."

Crushing and reshaping my pillow, I had just closed my eyes when I heard a whisper in my spirit. "Pray for an angel for Lisa," it said—and I bolted upright as, on the heels of what I hadn't yet processed, a second "thought" followed the first. "Pray she does *not* go through the tunnel."

The hairs on my arms stood straight up. Pray for an angel? Don't go through the tunnel?

"Scotty!" I nearly shouted, shaking my husband's shoulder. "Scotty," I pleaded, knowing it wasn't his fault if he couldn't wake up on demand but praying he'd come awake soon. "We need to pray for Lisa," I cried, as my husband bolted upright, too. We were to pray for an angel, I quickly explained, and Lisa was not to go through that tunnel.

Scotty stared at me for several seconds before he took my hand. "She'll be okay, Babe," he said, as we bowed our heads.

Though I couldn't stop shaking, together we recalled God's promises—told him we'd read his Word, and we believed that Word when it said his angels encamp around those who fear him. We also reminded ourselves that he takes care of his own. Then, Scotty fell back to sleep while I rested my head in the crook of his arm *and* listened to the pendulum on the wall clock mark time in another room.

Five minutes after midnight, the phone rang—and, picking up the receiver, I heard my daughter's voice. "Mom!" she cried. She sounded as if she'd been running. "Mom!" she repeated, breathless. "There was an *angel* on my train!"

Numbed by my daughter's announcement, I found it impossible to form a single word.

"There was no one else at my bus stop, Mom," she said, "when I left work." But when she'd transferred to the Metro? "He was on the train!" When she first spotted him just sitting there, she'd felt frightened. She'd boarded at the end of the line; where had this person come from?

"But then he looked at me, Mom, and he had the most beautiful eyes." I envisioned my daughter smiling; her voice had grown calm. "I've never seen eyes like his before, and then he started to speak, but it didn't seem like he could hear." Just a man who was deaf, she'd thought at first. "But he wasn't just a man," Lisa said.

I wanted to speak, but I couldn't. And now Lisa was saying he'd told her that her life had been difficult. He was right; it had been. But it was going to become good; she wasn't to be afraid.

"Lisa . . ." I began, trying not to cry and quietly laughing with relief and wondering how God had done such a miraculous thing.

"And, Mom?" Lisa still hadn't quite caught her breath, but now she was crying and laughing, too. "I got off the train. You know where."

I certainly did; it gave me the chills just to imagine. "And I started toward the tunnel." Lisa paused. "But something kept saying, 'Don't go through the tunnel. *Don't* go through the tunnel.'"

Don't go through the tunnel? I felt as if I'd stopped breathing. My mouth dry, I began to tell my daughter about the prayers we'd just prayed. I told her I loved her and that God loved her so much, too—and then, when we were both too tired to talk, I placed the receiver back down where it belonged. *Pray for an angel and don't go through the tunnel?* Had God actually put an angel on my daughter's train? Could the tunnel incident have been imagination or coincidence?

Not until several days had passed did I receive what, for me, was my answer—and only then did I wholly understand God had, in fact, set a watch over my child.

Scotty had been in Washington for a meeting where he'd purchased a newspaper for me—and on a middle page, I read the report. A rapist who'd eluded the police for months had finally been arrested.

Just a stone's throw from the tunnel, only yards from my daughter's door.

20

Grandma's Calendar

Jesus did not let him, but said, "Go home to your family and tell them how much the Lord has done for you, and how he has had mercy on you."

Mark 5:19

Her fragile, floral teacup in the palm of my hand, I remembered the day she'd given me the only pretty dishes she'd ever owned—dishes purchased with tip money during the thirties when she'd worked a lunch counter in order to feed her children and herself. "I want you to have these, Nancy Grace," she'd said. "I don't want them going to anybody else."

"I do love her," I said, "and I should go out there. But, Scotty, I'm so busy."

My husband gave me that look that says, "You're digging pretty deep for an excuse, Babe."

Well, let him look. My calendar was full. Maybe I could just call her.

"She hasn't had a very good time of it," Scotty said. "She needs you."

No, she hadn't had a good time of it. Not as a child when life was lean; not as a young wife and, then, single with children and, eventually, back again with my grandfather. And, now, not a very good time of it because this same grandfather's death had again left her alone.

"You're right," I said, "I need to do this."

So I prepared to pack—and made lists. My daughter's school would want to know I was leaving. There were neighbors to notify, and the Newcomers Club had expected I'd help with the brunch. Had I remembered to tell Julie I couldn't lead Monday's discussion? Should I call someone else instead?

I collected luggage, dropped it onto the bed. Gathering clothing and cosmetics, I glanced at the summer picture of Grandma with that glow on her face that always appeared when she cared for her garden, but I also had a garden to tend.

Parting the curtains, I looked out the window and discovered sunrise had begun to make a morning. Well, at least I would have good traveling weather.

In the hallway, I tucked maps into my purse; I would cross three states. I hoped the roads would not be crowded, hoped there wouldn't be convoys of eighteen-wheelers in front of me. I caught Scotty on his way to the kitchen. "You will water my flowers and you won't forget to feed my cat?"

"Yes, Mommy." Scotty grinned. "I'll water what needs watering and feed what needs to be fed—if I don't get mixed up." He was laughing.

"Funny," I said, thinking he was often very funny— but not today. Today, I'd been scheduled to speak to a gathering at church, but I had canceled on them. Grandma's note had seemed so gloomy. It wasn't like her. Maybe Scotty could go with me later? Grandma was crazy about him.

"Scotty," I said, turning to suggest we call her—but he was already on his way to my Honda carrying my bags to my trunk.

"Don't forget gymnastics," I reminded, as my pre-teen drifted from her room.

"Stop fussing, Mom," she said, nodding.

Was I fussing or did I just have a great deal on my mind? How would they function without me? I turned to tell Lisa I could stay home, but she was giving me one of her looks. Okay, so I hovered, and the two of them would do fine. But what about square dancing? I'd said I'd bring dessert.

"Scotty, what about square dancing?"

"Took care of it," he said. "Called them yesterday."

Well, there went that excuse. *And you are making excuses, Nancy,* I said to myself. None of this busyness was all that important. *Truth is, you don't like leaving home; you're not good at change; you dread driving alone.*

There were few eighteen-wheelers. Beyond the highway, mountains glistened with the hint of winter. Before long, there would be snow. Grandma loved the mountains. If she had come to our house instead, I'd have taken her to see them. But her arthritis had been acting up; she almost always felt better in her own home.

In western Montana, I spotted a farm. What wondrous stories Grandma had told me about growing up in the country. Stories about pet horses and faith and love. Would I have understood anything about either topic if I hadn't spent time with Grandma—watching her study her Bible, listening as she read aloud to me?

Entering Idaho, I imagined the Garner homesteads south of the highway. Grandma had given me both literal pictures and word pictures of my great-grandfather's house and mill. She'd told me of troubled times, her father's goodness, growing up without a mother, and how God had gotten her through. Though my knees were knobby and I often felt in the way and homely, Grandma had made me feel good about me at her house. "You're so very special," she'd say, giving me one of her hugs. Because of her, I could stand today before other women to encourage them as well. Scotty was right; I needed to spend time with Grandma. I needed to tell her again what an impression she'd made and how much she meant to me.

"But the timing," I groaned, nearing the Washington-Idaho border . . . and imagining my husband's laughter. "Oh, sure, the whole world will be in limbo while you're away," he'd say.

Okay, he was right; nothing would actually come to a standstill in my absence. The brunch would go on without me and so would the women and their discussion. I just hoped they wouldn't be discussing me.

Pulling into Spokane, I remembered all the overnights at Grandma's cottage-like house. I remembered playing jacks on her front sidewalk, calling "All-ee All-ee outs in free" over the tiny rooftop, digging red potatoes for suppers that always included watermelon pickles and jam. And, afterwards, drying dishes in an apron she saved for special times, snuggling into my bed in the cellar near the wood furnace to read books she'd given me, feeling the warmth of the pressed flannel sheets she'd tuck up under my chin.

Rounding the corner and entering the familiar neighborhood, I could almost taste the grapes from Grandma's backyard—the ones that once grew deep purple on the arbor where we helped ourselves to samples, made clothespin dolls, and read about the northern lights, Wendy, and Peter Pan.

I hadn't even come to a complete stop in her gravel drive when she appeared, her arms thrown wide and her homemade apron and cotton dress pressed. She hadn't donned her church hat but, for a minute, I wished she had. I wondered if, in the wardrobe in the basement, I might again find the jaunty collection in grosgrain, flowers, velvet, and felt. Did she wear them anymore? Had she tossed the ones that once "belonged" to me?

As if playing hopscotch, she made her way across the thin strip of lawn. Wearing patched hose and sensible shoes, her softly permed hair whiter than I'd remembered, she came only to my chin. At ninety-plus, her face was still as pretty as a girl's. Her cheeks were pink, her perfume blending with the parsnips I suspected had already begun to boil at the back of her old-fashioned stove.

"Oh . . . oh . . ." she kept saying, hugging me as if I were a child again. She was so glad to see me, she kept repeating, steering me through the back door and up the freshly painted, not-so-sturdy wooden stairs.

"Oh . . . oh . . ." I heard her singing, as I deposited my belongings in her room with the twin beds where she wanted me to spend the night in the bed next to hers.

Turning to pass through the den, I touched the worn keys of Grandpa's upright piano and glanced at my tote full of lists and letters to be answered. I doubted I'd sleep; I had mental checking to do.

I'd pulled out my chair at the drop-leaf wooden table—thinking how still this house was and how full of talk and laughter mine would be—when I spotted Grandma's calendar. And taking a closer look at the lone, filled square, all that I'd thought so important paled as I read the three scribbled words: "Nancy's coming today."

We lost Grandma the following year and, for a while, nothing mattered. I'd take long walks alone and remember—because I'd believed my own calendar was so terribly important—I'd nearly missed a promise made to

Grandma. My grandma at whose feet I once sat, my grandma with picture books at her house and her telling me everything she believed about God. My grandma and the last precious time we spent making chocolate milk-shakes for supper while I told her how much she had given me, how she had planted good seeds in my heart—how she had made me feel wanted and loved.

But then one morning as I watched a sunrise make a morning on my own garden, I remembered something she had taught me. Gathering a bouquet of the flowers she had loved so, I knew one day I would again hear her singing where the safe place was—the place where Grandma would be writing on her heavenly calendar, "Nancy's coming today."

21

Bingo! Every Tuesday

Instead, speaking the truth in love, we will in all things
grow up into him who is the Head, that is, Christ.

Ephesians 4:15

Winter in Montana might be heaven on earth for a skier,
but for someone who grew up with beach sand between
her toes? Someone who thought heaven would have an
ocean? No, Montana winters didn't exactly look like or
feel a bit like heaven. So when Scotty's work moved us
back to where we'd met and married, I was grateful for
friendships to renew, but I'd made up my mind to hole
up in the house for the six months it would be snowing.
I didn't care, actually, if there were things going on
beyond our road; I had my writing, my music, my books.
In fact, once I'd resigned myself to staying indoors, it
became something more than resignation; I decided I'd
been born to this, liked the alone time, liked the idea
that I had an excuse in the form of dizzying drifts. Had

an excuse, that is, until the morning my husband's uncle telephoned.

Pushing ninety, Scotty's Uncle Lin still shoveled his neighbor's walk. He still chopped and gathered wood for the wood stove. He still thought winters were heavenly. He also thought that going to the senior center every Tuesday was just about the best thing in our town to do. He'd help his wife get ready—because getting around by then wasn't easy for her—and then he'd bundle her into the car, drive the dozen or so blocks, and get her settled at the table with the other "girls." That business dealt with, he'd make his way up front to call Bingo numbers. Because he was old-fashioned, Uncle Lin also decided it wasn't good for me to be alone. "That husband of yours travels too much," he'd say, and some days I'd agree. Still, it went with the job; we'd made up our minds a long time ago to do what we needed to do. "Nope," his uncle would say anyway, "just isn't right; you need to get out more; not good you're staying home."

The answer to what he saw as my problem?

"Bingo!" he said. "We play every Tuesday. You just come on into town, eat a bite of lunch with us. You'll see." They served up chicken-fried steak, he said, and mashed potatoes with lots of gravy. "You'll like the 'girls,' too," he added, with an enthusiastic flicker in his eye.

I tried all the excuses I could think of, but nothing was dissuading him.

"I don't want to play Bingo with the 'girls,'" I'd groaned on the phone to Scotty.

"Then tell him."

"No!" I couldn't do that. Make him think I thought they were old? Make him feel like I didn't appreciate his concern or that I believed chicken-fried steak wasn't good enough? "No," I told my husband. I'd figure something else out.

116

"Babe," Scotty said, "wouldn't it just be better to tell them the truth and then—"

I shook my head; he just didn't get it sometimes. I glared at the telephone. No, it wouldn't be better to tell the truth. Not this time. This time, I'd say I *could* go . . . but then, something might come up.

And something did. The very Tuesday morning I was dreading, the day I'd said I'd visit their senior center? Heaven on earth began again to appear out front before daybreak. Snow in the form of flakes the size of saucers. Snow so thick with winter I couldn't see my closest neighbor's house, let alone the road I'd need to travel to make it all the way into town.

"Hooray!" I whooped, sincerely grateful for the drifts building at the end of our drive; grateful that there was absolutely no way I could traverse it; grateful that all I needed to do now was to call and say, "I'm so very sorry." I'd also add that I'd try to go some other time, but there were drifts as high as a house at our house. On my way to the phone, I grinned at the thought of my cozy chair by the fire, a good book, and a pot of berry tea.

"Not coming?" Uncle Lin shouted over the phone, his hearing aid obviously giving him the predictable trouble. "Going to miss the games and lunch? Red Jell-O today," he said, "and homemade pie. Worked in the kitchen myself last night just to get it ready."

I told him the pie sounded very tempting, but there wasn't even the remotest possibility. However, the third time I said "Sorry" I did feel just a twinge of guilt, even though the road was simply beyond me—"And those drifts—"

"Well, all I know," my husband's uncle said, "is that he travels too much, and it isn't right that you should miss out."

117

Aloud, I agreed with him completely, made my voice sound just as disappointed as it could sound—even though, inside, I felt like singing.

When we hung up, I filled my London cup with tea and boiling water, gathered my books, decided against the fire in the stove, and started for my office up under the eaves on the top floor. From there I would look out at the mountains—the place where all the deep-powder types would be thinking they were blessed, though I would be the one rejoicing.

I was in the middle of my rejoicing and also in the middle of a writing, when I heard a noise I'd never heard before. A sort of whirring. A rumble, really—the kind we sometimes overheard when snow slid off the cedar-shake roof. Only today nothing could possibly be sliding; it was too cold; it was still piling up, up there.

Again, I heard it. This time whatever it was had also begun to do a shriek and then a whining.

"Good grief!" I blurted, heading for the room next door. "What in the world?" I began to utter as I dashed downstairs. Throwing open the library blinds, I spotted the figure of a man swaddled in one of those suits that makes him look like an astronaut. Swaddled from head to toe with only his eyes and glasses showing, eyes with a flicker in them, eyes belonging to my husband's Uncle Lin. In front of him, a machine was blowing snow to both sides of our driveway, blowing a path exactly where I would normally back out my car—if I were planning to leave my snug home.

Squinting in an attempt to get a better look in the glare of the too-white sky, I saw—in Uncle Lin's truck—someone wrapped in blankets and a jacket. It was Frances. Sitting comfy like the grandma in a cherished childhood book. Sitting there waiting while the engine ran.

"Sitting there waiting for *me?*"

It took me less than one minute to find my own jacket and boots. Another to jerk Scotty's ski hat down over my ears and hair. A third minute to throw open the garage door and shout, "Why are *you* here? What in the world are you *doing?*" Beyond my husband's uncle, I could see more clearly now, and I didn't like what I saw at all! He'd blown a path through the impassable drift! My driveway was practically bare all the way to the county-plowed road.

"No!" I wanted to shout. "Put it back! I'm *not* going."

Uncle Lin had steered his snowblower around behind me. Now he was coming back and grinning. I didn't have to see his entire face to know that; I had only to look at his eyes. Then, switching the engine off and turning back around to look squarely at me, he pulled down the scarf he'd wrapped around his mouth, nodded, and said, "Nope! It's not right you bein' alone and missin' out on Bingo!" His grizzled grin grew wide, while the snow around us frosted his cheeks and chin. "Figured we get this driveway cleared, and you won't have to miss any of it. Not the games *or* the mincemeat pie." He chuckled, and I just stared. *Babe, wouldn't it be better just to tell the truth?* I could hear Scotty saying. The truth. *If only I'd told—*

"So," Uncle Lin said, as he ran his snowblower up a ramp he'd made from salvaged boards, "we'll just give you time to get yourself properly dressed. Won't hurt us any to sit. Then we'll go on ahead, and you follow." He nodded. "And then," he said, his grin full of fun, "Bingo!"

"Bingo," I said, with a lot less enthusiasm. I'd be ready in two jerks of a lamb's tail, I told him, listening to his laughter and thinking what a special man this was. Thinking that he probably hadn't told a fib in all his going-on-ninety years. Thinking about all the people who loved him in his neighborhood, in his church, at the senior center.

And that afternoon, playing Bingo next to Frances and the other "girls" and dining on red Jell-O, chicken-fried steak, and mashed potatoes? I was given a taste of what my second childhood would be like. A childhood where people gathered together and shared pie midday and told one another the truth—even sometimes when it was painfully blunt. And later, as I prepared to negotiate the road home, I made a promise I could keep: "I can't say for sure that I'll make it every Tuesday, but I'll try."

And I did. And when I did, I was glad that I did. What began as something dreaded had turned out to be a blessing: I'd been given an afternoon with a good man and his good wife and their good friends—special people not only telling the truth in love but sharing their concern for others and expressing gratitude for the life each was living and had lived.

Bingo!

22

Mostly a
Moving Experience

Even the sparrow has found a home . . .

Psalm 84:3a

In less than 26 years, I have walked through 15 relocations. Several of those exoduses we saw as instant blessings. Others tested my faith; they were difficult. And, in
my mind, the worst? The migration we agreed to for a
pay raise of $2000.00 a year—before taxes. In those days,
that seemed like a great deal of money, and we needed
it. It wasn't just the two of us; we had a daughter in high
school who would need all sorts of things in her senior
year—not to mention her desire to go to college. So we
said yes to the promotion that would move us from New
Mexico, packed up our belongings, did our level best to
console our daughter and—driving two U-haul trucks

and both of us towing automobiles—began what would become an extraordinary journey.

Only *after* we'd reached Pennsylvania did we hear the news for which we'd not prepared ourselves. The mortgage interest rates had taken a flying leap; we would no longer be paying just under 6 percent; instead, we'd be looking at 17.

And I lost it. There was no way, I told my husband; I didn't have to be a genius to know we were doomed. The payments on our Albuquerque house had been just about more than we could handle, and now we'd be looking at what amounted to a double payment and on just $2000.00 more per year—before taxes?

"It'll work out, Babe," Scotty said. "It always does."

I wanted to tell him that it didn't always. In fact, if I looked back and brought up all the old baggage, I could tell him just a whole lot about things that hadn't worked out, how we'd blown it, missed it, and how God was not with us but with someone else who'd listened more closely, drawn nigh more often, prayed more fervently.

But I didn't tell my spouse; I told God. Like the persistent woman before the judge, I went to the Lord, and I pleaded. I told him I knew for a fact that we weren't going to be able to do this. I reminded him I no longer had a teaching job, that he'd called me to write, that I was making $37.00 a year—and this was just going to turn out to be our worst mistake. I told him all of that and more, but I heard nothing.

Meanwhile, a realtor came to pick us up and to lay out the inventory from which we could make a selection. And I cried. We'd lived like that once before—in a neighborhood where I was afraid to let my daughter out of the house. I'd already had my experiences with the wrong side of town, where we suspected there were drugs on the street and rodents at the neighbor's and with our roof about to peel right off the house.

Our realtor was sympathetic. A kind man, actually—but there was just so much he could show us in our price range.

So we continued the search—with Scotty in the front seat reading listings and me in the backseat pleading with God. I wanted to call it *prayer*—but it was begging. We needed a house, and we needed it quick. We also needed payments we could handle. We were going to be subsidized by Scotty's employer while we lived in the Holiday Inn with an unhappy daughter and a dog, but they wouldn't be putting us up forever. When our time was up, we'd be on our own, and I was *not* going to live in the park with a bench for a bed and with my yard encompassing the whole outdoors.

Three days of searching, and we found nothing habitable, nothing that didn't make me shudder, nothing that even remotely resembled a fixer-upper. Worse, it was time for Scotty to join a car pool for the drive to his new office. "But you'll find something, Babe," he said. He didn't pat me on the head, but he gave me that look that said he knew I'd be a good sport and that everything would work out.

Meanwhile, our real estate agent was about at the end of his rope. He'd also come to the end of his "affordable" list. "I can talk to some friends at the bank," he said. The man drew his chin through his hand. "They might consider giving you a loan at just 15 percent."

Just? So now maybe I could also buy groceries on occasion? I shook my head; there had to be something out there, I said. I couldn't believe God would impress upon us to make this move and then not provide us with—at the very least—passable housing. Hadn't people prayed for us in New Mexico? Hadn't the Lord confirmed with his Word that we were to do this? Hadn't I "seen" in my spirit and during my prayer time glimpses of what he had planned? "No," I said, watching our realtor shrug and shake his head. "I don't think we can pay even 15 percent, but we're also not living in a place where I have to worry about my daughter."

For the next several days, we drove up one street and down another. Searching, hoping, thinking just maybe we'd see something that hadn't yet made it into his MLS book. Then one morning—while I sat across from his desk with my feet firmly planted and determined that we were going to find what we needed—an agent we hadn't yet met crossed the room. "I've been listening," she said. She nodded first at me and then at our flustered agent. "And I think this might be something." She handed a listing to her colleague, smiled at me, and backed away.

He hadn't thought . . . but maybe. Our agent shrugged. We could go look and see. He'd pull his car around front; I could hop in the front seat this time, and we'd go back to the part of the town that was beyond us.

Driving past a farm with cows and horses, I noted how lovely the trees were and that there were ducks on a pond and a sign marking a reservoir not far away. I spotted the high school we'd been told was the best; I wanted my daughter to go there. At a tiny milk store, there were customers coming outside to their cars with glass bottles of milk. One sign said, "homemade ice cream," and another announced they were planning a country fair.

Then we turned a corner, started down a tree-lined road with lovely houses tucked back a ways and with split-rail fences and daylilies growing profusely—and over the top of a knoll where we began to descend into a clearing, I saw it. "That's it!" I said, noting the startled look on my driver's face and thinking he'd already decided I was a client he'd never forget. One that might well push him into an early retirement.

"That's it?" He was looking at me sideways, his face wrinkled up in a frown.

I nodded.

"You haven't seen the inside."

I didn't need to.

"Difficult people to deal with," he said.

Was he talking about Scotty and me?

"House has been sitting empty for months."

"I don't care," I said. "I want to see it."

At the front door, he found the key; I stepped in—and discovered the inside wasn't what we'd thought we needed. The woman had gone crazy with the colors, one of each, every room disconnected from the next by wall-papers and chartreuse and pink. But it had wrapped itself around me; I wanted to take my shoes off and put up my feet. I was home.

Back at the realtor's office, however, they explained I probably wasn't. The sellers had vacated, moved themselves and their belongings down South, and said they would entertain nothing but full offers. Anything less and they weren't to be disturbed. Meanwhile, buyers had come, had tried offering just a little less—and the owner had threatened to throw them out if he had to.

I shrugged but not in resignation. This was the house; I knew it. I called Scotty; he came back to the Holiday Inn. He'd go look, he said, but if the realtor thought we didn't have a chance?

We hadn't even driven up the drive when Scotty nodded. "Yes, Babe, this is it for me, too," he said.

So, back to the office we went. "We're going to make an offer," we said.

"A full offer?" Our realtor straightened his coffee-stained tie.

We shook our heads. We weren't trying to pull something; we weren't asking to have the house for anything less just because we'd gotten greedy; we just didn't have any more money than we had. And with the interest rates the way they were . . .

Our realtor called his boss. "We've had nothing but trouble with this man," the broker said. "But—" he looked directly at me. "If you feel this strongly, I'll go there myself . . . and we'll see."

He'd go there? Weren't the owners living somewhere in the Carolinas?

"Here, actually," he said. He didn't know why, but he'd gotten a call that very morning. For some reason, they were back in town. Just until tomorrow, though, and then they would be leaving. "So," he said, "I've made an appointment to see them. They won't come here; I'll have to go to the house. They want me to come tonight."

Inside, I felt like crying. Outside, I smiled; Scotty smiled, too. The broker thought we were nuts—but he would try, and that's all we could ask.

That night, however, we'd begun to wish we'd asked a lot more questions. If we didn't get this house, what then? If the seller said "No!" to our offer, should we try to make the payments on the place? Should I see if I could find work? What about that bank that might let us have money for "just" 15 percent?

For two hours, we asked ourselves all the questions. We also walked the dog, watched the moon come up, discovered fireflies, wondered how much longer, reminded ourselves that we needed to let our friends and family know where we were, prayed our daughter would adjust to this move . . . prayed God would give us this house and that he would do so tonight.

By 11:30 P.M., we'd heard nothing; we were weary and prayed out. There was nothing more we could do; we'd simply go to bed. If God gave us the house, then we'd praise him. If he did not, we'd still praise—and continue to look.

At 11:45, Scotty reached over and took my hand. "I think we need to pray again," he said.

I agreed.

So we began to pray that our broker would be given favor with the people he'd agreed to talk to. We prayed God would give us peace sufficient to sleep. We also prayed over each room of that house—walking through it in our minds and hearts—when something began to happen, something I'd never before experienced. I began to "see"—with my eyes closed. To "see" something flapping, black, and slimy. Something around the base of the house in the shrubbery beds. Something that came up out of the dirt, encircled the foundation, slapped like fins against the concrete—and a chill began to overwhelm me.

"Scotty!" I cried. "I just saw—" and I began to tell him, and as I told, he began to pray all the more fervently. We prayed against whatever it was that thought it had the power to frighten; we prayed against any evil thing that thought itself more powerful than God; we prayed against anything that had planted itself around or inside that house. And as we continued to pray, something else began to appear. Where I had "seen" the black slimy things, a bright light began to shine. A light that surrounded the foundation and, in the light, beautiful snow-white lilies began to displace the gruesome forms. The house filled with a light in all the windows, light that warmed not only the house but me.

Just seconds before midnight, the phone began to ring in our room. "I don't understand any of this," the voice at the other end said. It was the broker. "But you two have yourselves a house."

We had a house? We had *the* house? "Praise God! Praise God!" we cried. And then we slept like babies; we slept knowing we would have a real home.

The following morning, we received our confirmation. This house was not only *the* house, but God had worked a miracle, and he'd done so in the presence of our skeptical realtor. Pacing the floor with his cigarette dangling from between his fingers, he'd occasionally glance at us, but for several minutes he said nothing. Then, finally—while we looked at him and at one another—he pulled out a chair. "I don't understand any of this," he said, obviously unnerved. "But we sat for nearly two hours . . . with the seller threatening to throw me out." The broker cleared his throat. "He was mad as . . . said he'd already told us the deal. No lowering the price, no bargains. But then, just before midnight, his wife opened the door." She'd been waiting all that time in the next room. "She looked at him," the broker said.

And I looked at Scotty. Just before midnight? When we were praying and I saw—?

"And this is what she said." The broker took a long drag on his smoke. "'I don't know why,' she said, looking at her husband. 'But *God* wants them to have this house.'"

God wanted us to have the house? He *had* been doing the leading?

"So," the agency owner said, "this is the deal." They were going to accept the price we could pay, and we could move in the following week; they'd also decided they'd carry most of the loan themselves, and we could have it at 13 percent.

"13—?"

The broker nodded.

The balance?

He'd get a friend at the bank to cover at 15. He took out his calculator, and Scotty did the same, and within minutes we were looking at payments we could handle, payments that would keep us within our budget, payments that would put us in the house God had selected for us. Not only would the sparrows out back have a brand-new home—once we'd unpacked all the feeders and seed—but we would have a real home, too. God had done it again, just as he'd done so many times before. He'd walked us through yet another test, showed us how much he cares and closely watches. Guided us by the touch of his hand.

23

An Uncommon Communion

They devoted themselves to the apostles' teaching and
to the fellowship, to the breaking of bread and to prayer.

Acts 2:42

We would be moving again. Leaving the home I couldn't
bear to leave, turning our truck and our household
goods again to face the East Coast, driving Scotty's old
truck cross-country, saying good-bye to the place where
my heart knew the first home I had known for years.
Leaving friends, leaving the mountains—and for more
than a month I had grieved. I understood, of course, this
was something we needed to do; it was a decision we'd
made for the good of my husband and for his career.
Not only that, he was doing the best he knew to do, taking care of us in the only way that he could. Furthermore, our daughter needed us to be there and not here.

"But it's so hard," I cried one morning on my knees and watching the sun fill the golden skylight. "I can't bear this," I breathed. It wasn't just this move; I'd also had another surgery, one that had literally laid me up almost completely—while Scotty had been asked again to travel. While I stayed behind in Montana with my foot and leg wrapped and barely able to get around my house on rented crutches, Scotty would work first in South Carolina and then Washington, D.C. "I'm sorry, Babe," he'd said when he'd put his suitcases down at our front door and hugged me, "but there's nothing else I can do." Of course there wasn't. I knew that; I understood. Understood my husband's reasons, that is. But God's? Those I questioned. Did he not see that I'd been napping on my neighbor's bed so someone could keep an eye on me? Did he not understand I couldn't even get to the grocery store or church without someone offering to drive? And now—on my knees—possible I wouldn't even be able to pull myself up again to stand?

"No, I really do not understand," I said—and heard the thought, *communion.*

"I want you to take communion," he said.

Communion? Where? When? Yes, I knew the Lutheran church we'd attended on occasion did serve communion every Sunday morning, but this was Monday. Did he want me to wait seven days? And if that was the case, how did he expect me to get myself there? My friend Donna had been carting me from my home to the store, and my friend Teri had even taken me to her house where I could rest. But ask them to drive me to a church that wasn't even their own?

"Communion," I heard again. Not only that, there was the slightest impression—slight enough that it nearly went right over my head—that I was to go to a storefront church all the way across town. A church I'd never attended, a church where I would recognize no one. Surely he wasn't saying, "Go there."

For the rest of the week, I slept, read, prayed, waited for a friend to come to visit or to take me for a ride in her car. Daily, Scotty would call, but he could do nothing for me—except to say he also didn't understand how I was going to take communion when our town was covered with snow, and I wasn't to drive, and the weatherman was saying, "Stay home."

It wasn't until Saturday evening that I heard in my spirit again that I was to do this thing that God had called me to do. It also wasn't until Saturday evening that I decided I *could* get *myself* to the church. No, it wouldn't be easy. Fear and trepidation gripped me when I thought about driving Scotty's old truck. Still, it was the only vehicle we had that could go through snow and over roads with ice.

Later that night, I laid out my clothes. Hobbling from our closet to our bed, I prepared for the following morning. It wouldn't be easy, and I wouldn't be making an impression on the world of fashion. I'd wear clothing I could put myself into; I would wear a shoe on one foot and wrap the other. I wasn't to get the dressings wet.

Sunday morning, I bundled for the cold and, with the help of crutches, climbed up into the driver's seat and slammed the door. Backing out of our drive, I wondered if I'd lost my mind completely. None of the neighbors were out on the road; normally, even Scotty would have suggested we stay home; but God had said . . .

Just as they did every Sunday morning, the Lutheran congregation took communion, and I went forward. My going was slow, but the people were patient. Impatience, however, began to stir within me. At the communion rail, I had this niggling feeling; I wasn't in the right place nor was this to be the time. Something had stirred in my spirit, something that said, "Not here, not now." The

communion in this particular church and at this hour—
not to mention the time it had taken to get here—had
all been for naught?

Back home, I went to my knees again to ask, "Why?"
Why, when I'd tried to obey, had God not been there for
me?

Again the thought of the storefront church across
town came to mind. He actually wanted me to go to a
church with a handful of people? To a place where I
would know no one? What if I couldn't drive that far?
What if the snow continued and the ice became worse?
What if I couldn't manage the several steps from the
curb up to their door?

Grabbing Scotty's parka from the closet nearest the
garage, I leaned on my crutch, slipped first into one
sleeve and then the other, headed again for the truck—
and began the drive I hoped would *not* be my last.

When I reached the church, there were no lights—no
Sunday evening service? Obviously I hadn't heard God
at all. Peering through the passenger's window, I spotted on the door of the tiny building the hours when they
would meet. "Wednesday evening," I read.

"Okay," I breathed, sitting stiff and upright again at
the wheel and praying I'd get home in what was becoming an even heavier snow than I'd anticipated. "Still," I
whispered, "I'm coming back somehow midweek."

On Wednesday evening, I left my house early; I didn't
know how the roads would be; all that I'd heard were
the warnings to stay home.

When I arrived at the church, I was able to park where
I'd parked on Sunday evening. Directly in front of the
building, directly in front of the several stairs and steps
that led to the glass-front door.

Inside, there was just me and one teenager reading
her Bible. When I limped toward where she was sitting,
she looked up.

"Hi," I said. "I guess I'm a little bit early."

She smiled, nodded. "The others will be here before long," she said, before turning back around to read.

Normally, I like a little space between myself and the other guy, but that night I wanted to sit close to where she was sitting. Maybe then—when the others arrived—they wouldn't notice they didn't know me. Maybe they'd think I had come with her, that I actually had a church-member friend. And pretty soon, several did begin to wander in, laughing and talking with one another and seeming not to notice I was a stranger. Meanwhile, the girl—once she'd finished what she was doing—turned to say she was glad to meet me, asked if I'd been here before, said she really liked this church—and I began to think I liked it, too. There was something sweet here, something I could feel but couldn't put my hands on.

Several minutes later, a young couple came to where the girl and I were sitting. The woman was with child, her husband handsome and tall. "Hi!" they chimed. "Are you new here?"

I nodded and told them I was. I glanced around the church, noticed it was beginning to fill.

"Well," the young woman said, "my husband and I are the worship leaders." She grinned and pressed the palms of her hands to her swollen belly. "But as you can see, I'm very pregnant, so we won't be leading for a while." Her husband wrapped an arm around her shoulders, and we talked for a few minutes more before they turned to visit with friends. Just then a man came dashing into the sanctuary from behind me and started up the aisle. A man with a basket and bread.

"Oh . . ." I said, the "Oh" barely uttered as I turned again to look at the teenager sitting beside me. "I see you take communion on Wednesday evenings."

"We never have before," she said, shrugging, "and I've been coming here for about eight or nine months."

They never had before? I glanced again at the man who was heading back up the aisle now and exiting through the doors through which he'd entered.

Meanwhile, the young couple who'd been the worship leaders had finished milling around. They were coming to where I sat, sitting down close—though not beside me—and the man who'd delivered the basket of bread was returning. This time with a tray and the cup.

Feeling every hair on my arms respond, I turned this time to face the expectant couple. The teenager just hadn't been paying attention, I told myself. They no doubt took communion on some Wednesdays. Maybe she'd just missed a couple of weeks. "I see you have communion on Wednesdays," I said to the worship leaders.

The puzzled man shrugged. "No," he said. He turned to look at his wife who was also shaking her head. "We've been coming here for years," she was saying, "but we've never before had communion on a Wednesday evening."

I heard myself swallow, heard my heart and a ringing in my ears—as the pastor walked back up the aisle, studied the members of his congregation—and shook his head. Then, in a voice filled with peace *and* expectation, he said, "I don't *know* what's going on." He paused. "But while I was sitting in my study, the Lord spoke. There will be no message this evening. We're simply to praise and worship—and then he wants communion served."

Communion? He did want me to take it, and he wanted me to take it here. In this place, this very Wednesday evening. In the middle of a snowstorm and with my husband away and my future seeming bleak and wondering why I was the one forsaken, he'd said "Communion" not only to me but to this man. Communion with the bread that symbolized Christ, the food for my soul. Communion, that I might relinquish all that I had and all that I'd hoped. Communion with the cup, *the* reminder that I could trust him. Communion, that

I might turn my eyes back again to him—and understand that *he* alone was in control of all that seemed out of control. That he was not only watching and directing but that his reasons were good.

I could make this move, and I would also make it back to my home across town. I would pack and say goodbye to special friends, to the home I thought I could not leave, to all the dreams I'd dreamed—because he loved not only my husband but me. To prove it, he'd spoken to the heart of a pastor who not only listened but heard—and an uncommon communion on a Wednesday evening had been served.

24

"Next!"

Therefore encourage one another and build each other up, just as in fact you are doing.

1 Thessalonians 5:11

The waiting room was empty, stuffy, damp. While I'd tried to wait patiently, a receptionist had been scouring her post with something that smelled lethal, and now she'd wheeled on one heel, checked her functional watch, and over the top of my head bellowed, *"Ne-xt!"*

Next? I was the only patient in here! I considered snapping back, but I obediently sidestepped to a second slit of a window, instead.

"Why are *you* here?" the woman asked.

That's what I'm wondering, I kept to myself, wondering also why she couldn't have talked to me through the first window. "Mammogram," I said.

Donning a look of indifference, she demanded to know which doctor had referred me. "*His* name?" she asked. She hadn't yet looked directly at me.

"*Her* name's Jo-anne," I said. "Joanne Garrett." It was plainly written; why was I explaining?

As she forced my paperwork into a clip, I began to wonder if the woman might have chosen another line of work. Something like rounding up snakes? She'd moseyed to a filing cabinet to treat herself to an audible swallow of coffee, and now she'd returned—but she still hadn't looked directly at me.

"Whew, she's nasty," I breathed.

"Address for your doctor?" She'd again looked at her watch; obviously I was keeping her from something. A class in *How to Win Friends and Influence People* perhaps?

"On the form." I pointed.

"Humph," she said, yanking the paper to where I couldn't touch it. With her bottle of white-out in her hand, she'd blurred something on *my* insurance form. *My name?* I wanted to ask. Who put this woman in charge? I believed in equal employment—even for the irritating—"But this is stupid," I murmured, knowing my response was childish. Still, I couldn't help wishing I *could* be a child, one who didn't even *know* how to spell mammogram.

Finally, she was through with me. Obviously she'd read what she wanted to read and covered with white-out what she did not. "Have a seat," she said.

I wanted to say, "Your face will freeze that way if you don't watch out." I wanted to spill something on her sterile counter. Behind her back, I mimed, "You are rude. Rude, rude, rude." I drew a deep breath and hoped they wouldn't be taking my blood pressure today. I settled into a clammy chair and seized a copy of something full of nothing.

"Get a real job," I mumbled, glancing again at the hateful woman's back. Did she think I came here because I wanted to? Could she possibly believe I enjoyed being poked and pinched between plates of cold glass? Yes, for five years now they'd been saying the spot was "only calcium"—but I'm a creative thinker. I imagined this new doctor wouldn't measure up, had no interest in my medical history. We'd been moved again with Scotty's work; maybe my records hadn't yet caught up.

I bounced my foot the way I do when I'm "fuzzed up." Shuffling magazines, I discovered someone had blackened the teeth of some glamour girl and given her horns and a thin mustache. I couldn't help thinking how I'd delight in doing the same to that *other* woman.

"Ne-xt!" broke the silence for a second time—as an unsmiling, gowned-in-glaring-orange individual stepped into the waiting room. Possibly she was related to the trainer of snakes?

Clutching my purse, I followed the marching woman.

"Change in here," she ordered, jerking back a colorless curtain to reveal a space the size of the place where I store my dustpan and broom.

Donning a coral cover-up, I noticed it wasn't a bad color on me—but was it to open in the front or the back? I was in the middle of my wondering when I heard, "Ready, Mrs. Hoag, whenever you are"—but this voice was friendly, pleasant. There was the soft scent of lilacs and laughter as I drew the curtain back and discovered a girl about the age of my eldest daughter. "No hurry," she was saying now.

I thanked her and told her, "I'm ready." I also laughingly admitted I might have put the "gown" on backwards.

She laughed, said I'd done fine. And then she smiled directly at me—and I smiled, too, as I began to follow her down a buttercup-yellow hallway.

We'd gone through the routine questions and answers, with the technician explaining how many pictures she'd take. She also hoped I wouldn't be too uncomfortable, asked if this was "home."

Instantly, I told myself I wouldn't cry or go on and on about our most recent distressing move, but I did go on and on, told her I'd found this current setting was taking some getting used to. In one month, I'd been given a treadmill test, an EKG, told I might have ulcers, and was given yet another test for stress. Embarrassed by my spilling so much information, I wished we could get on with the exam—but the young technician had stepped away from her machine. She was telling me she was also missing the people she'd grown up with, the slower pace, evening walks with friends.

"They had time, made time," she said. Where she bought groceries, shopkeepers would ask how she was doing. She'd buy flowers, and a vendor would tuck in an extra. She'd visit a bakery, and they'd insist she sit a while. If she missed a day, merchants would miss her and tell her so.

Studying her face, I realized she was also close to tears. "But here," she said, "there is so much crime, all those drive-by shootings. We have a security system *and* a car alarm, but I don't dare go out alone." She shook her head. "Once it's dark, we don't even visit neighbors or drive into the city for fear—"

For fear? Instantly, I wondered, *Is that what's wrong with the receptionist?* Had she lived too long with *fear?* And the first technician? Had she become distrustful, too? Did they both—just like this younger woman *and* me—simply need a kind word, coffee with a friend, someone to give them a smile?

The mammogram all but forgotten, I counted all the relocations I had fought. "If it weren't for my faith, I'd have lost it four moves ago," I said. I even admitted I sometimes dreamed about "running folks off the road." Even this morning, I'd considered several ugly things I could tell that receptionist, I said.

The young technician laughed; she knew exactly what I was saying.

I told her I worked very hard at making time to pray, but what was it Scott Peck said? "Life is difficult." I glanced at my watch and apologized for taking her time—but she'd smiled, tugged a tissue from her pocket, dabbed her nose and eyes. "I'm in no hurry," she said. "Actually, I needed this. It takes me back to the kitchen table, my sister, my mom. Thanks," she said.

"No," I laughed, "I thank *you*—and so should that receptionist."

The mammogram completed, she said she'd have the doctor check my pictures. Within minutes, she had returned. "Only calcium." She smiled. "Everything's fine."

Relieved, I told her I hoped things would soon be fine for her, too.

She said they already were. "Yes," she said again, "I *really* needed this."

"Me, too," I said. It was good to remember we are legion—we women feeling cut off, distanced by circumstances, manipulated by choices not entirely our own.

I gathered my purse, swapped the coral gown for my navy T-shirt, exited the examining room—and told the receptionist, "Have a great day!"—as she offered a startled, cautious smile.

And then I started for home—knowing the traffic would be dreadful. I'd no doubt glance into my rearview mirror and discover an agitated commuter too close to my pickup truck. I'd consider braking and envision the other driver's startled expression. She'd raise a fist, I'd start to raise mine—but then I'd wonder if she was also going in for a bewildering examination, if she was also worried just a little, if she was feeling friendless, missing home.

Then, I'd ease into the right lane, instead, and whisper, "Ne-xt." And, giving the other woman room to pass, I would remember, "Life is difficult."

Not just for me, but for them.

25

The Miracle on Cristo Street

Do not think of yourself more highly than you ought, but rather think of yourself with sober judgment.

Romans 12:3b

"Don't go to San Juan; it isn't safe," our travel agent said.

"Safe or not, I have no choice," Scotty said with a shrug; and I shrugged, too—because, safe or not, I wanted to be with my husband. We'd be turning his business trip into a second honeymoon. I refused to give that up because of some ridiculous scare. But then we nearly missed our flight. In San Juan, we couldn't find our luggage. Officials were called; our porter couldn't make change. A cabby had started his meter; I tried explaining, but he'd opened my door, and now I sat alone, peering through dirty windows. I spotted my spouse; he wasn't happy; the cabby grinned.

At the curb, a uniformed man yanked bills from his pocket and slapped them into Scotty's hand. En route to our hotel, I wondered aloud if speaking only English could become a problem. Not only that, how did I honestly feel about these people? They were "different"—not like us. Might they even pick our pockets if we didn't watch them closely?

Entering a threadbare lobby, I nearly cried. The brochure had promised posh surroundings, but the hotel's restaurant had been closed by a board for some unhealthy reasons. We'd also been promised the second floor, but the ninth would have to do. I turned back the bedding, the sheets weren't clean. I checked the bathroom; I'd be wearing shoes. The building reeked; we were told chemicals were being used next door. Because of an oil spill, our beach had also been closed. Add to that a choking humidity, and I wanted to go home.

"You'll feel better after lunch," Scotty said and, over a bowl of potatoes, garlic, fish, and greens, I admitted I wouldn't spend much time in our hotel. I'd tour or shop. This would be an adventure, something to tell the kids. Meanwhile, Scotty grabbed a travel pouch he'd purchased. Though men in foreign countries carried them, I'd suggested it looked like a purse. I wondered if he should be carrying such a thing.

A guidebook had recommended waterfront shops, but after navigating blocks of buckled pavement, we'd grown weary. We stared at our map, turned it sideways and upside down.

"Scotty, do you actually *know* where we are?" I asked.

"Just keep walking, Babe," he said.

I didn't want to keep walking; we'd already walked for one wearisome hour, and it was *hot*. Couldn't we ask for directions? Couldn't he hide his "purse"?

"Babe, will you quit?" Scotty shook his head. "It's not a purse," he said.

Maybe not, but he wasn't used to carrying the thing, and what if someone who was desperate came up from behind us and took it?

At a filling station, we discovered we were on a street where there'd been a shootout between gangs and police. "How did you get here?" the attendant asked. "It isn't safe." We were to find the main street "at once."

I wanted to say, "See? I told you so." Instead, I thanked the man and so did my spouse—and then we tried to run. By now, however, we were exhausted; we would find a bus. Meanwhile, teens on roller blades and a man drinking from a paper bag began to gather around us. At a bus stop, a second man approached our bench then backed away. Across the street, bars covered doors and windows and concertina wire ringed parking lots.

"A jail?" I asked, thinking at least there'd be law enforcement in there.

"Protection for offices," Scotty said.

I wrapped my handbag straps around my arm twice and pointed. "*Your* purse is making me nervous, too," I said. What if he forgot he had it?

"Babe . . ."

I'd started to say something more when a smoke-spewing bus appeared. "Okay!" I exclaimed, feeling somewhat relieved. "Surely the driver will speak English!"

He didn't. Not only that, he didn't look pleased. I felt certain he hadn't wanted to stop for two Americans at all! "But at least we're off the street," I began, when I heard Scotty groan. He looked stricken. "The pouch," he was saying, "at the stop—"

The pouch at the stop? "We need to get off!" I squawked—first at the sullen-looking driver and then at my spouse as I bolted from my gummy, vinyl bench seat.

I pointed at the door.

145

The driver shook his head.

Playing charades, I pointed again and felt hot tears on my face.

The bus rumbled back into traffic. Not until we'd traveled six blocks did we come to a stop again—and jumping to the hot pavement, I clutched Scotty's hand. "Run! Please run!" I cried, but he was shaking his head. He was ashen. Was he sick? Having a heart attack? "Babe, I can't," he said.

"Well, *I* can!" I cried, feeling lightheaded but bolting forward.

I'd covered nearly a block when Scotty caught my hand.

"Babe, I'm sorry," he was saying, out of breath and looking beaten.

Sorry wasn't enough. "Our money . . . what if someone finds it?" I broke into a run again.

We hadn't gone a block when we spotted a vehicle they call "a Public"—which works a little bit like the car pools in this country—and I darted in front of the van.

The driver braked.

My words running into one another, I tried explaining.

The driver said nothing.

I pointed and pleaded; he just had to understand.

He shook his head.

"You don't . . . doesn't *anyone* speak English?"

"I do," I heard, as a delicate girl with dark eyes and dark hair leaned toward the passenger window.

"Please," I gasped. "Our money's at the bus stop, and we desperately need a ride."

For several seconds, the girl looked as if she might speak again, but she said nothing—and the van drove away.

Spinning around to look at Scotty, I noted he still didn't look well. He was exhausted. "The heat," he said.

But, in traffic again, we flagged down another driver, this one dressed in a U.S. Army uniform.

"*He'll* speak English!" I shouted. But he didn't. Not clearly. And although he'd unlocked his doors, he was also calling someone to say he'd picked up "two turistas." The whole time he talked, he watched us as if we were felons or thieves. He was asking someone to cover him, Scotty said. He would give us a ride, but he wouldn't trust us.

Within minutes, we were at the stop—but the purse was not.

We spent the entire evening canceling credit cards. I called my sister in Seattle; Scotty called colleagues in Albuquerque; the hotel manager called the police. After a day of traveling, a disappointing hotel, and now all of Scotty's money taken, we canceled dinner and fell into bed.

The following morning, however, we decided we wouldn't let this trip be ruined for us. We would go to the American Express office, pick up a new credit card, and use what cash I'd hidden. We told God we trusted that he'd missed none of what had happened, and we thanked him for whatever he was teaching us. Then we boarded another bus. As we made our way through the packed aisle, I did silently ask why he'd allowed such a thing—especially now. We hadn't talked much about it, but Scotty had been passed over for a dozen promotions. Though he'd tried believing God had something for him, he was struggling. "I guess I just don't have enough faith," he'd said. So why would God allow this to happen? Why, when I already had my doubts about trusting "these people"? Why, when my husband's faith was at an all-time low?

"This is how I *build* faith," I heard.

We lose our money and you build faith? I wanted to argue, but I joined Scotty for another walk instead.

In Old San Juan, where both tourists and locals mingle, we purchased gifts for neighbors and family; we photographed gardens and an eighteenth-century chapel overlooking the bay. We'd only just started up a long hill toward the three-hundred-year-old Church of San Jose—all the while wondering if we should turn back—when, suddenly, we heard a voice call, "Scott Hoag! Scott Hoag!"—as a delicate girl with dark eyes and dark hair emerged from a lovely lavender shop. The girl who'd understood English, the girl in the Public Van.

With joy on her face and my ears ringing, we met her in the middle of the street, and then she was steering us into her market—all the while laughing and talking and with browsers stopping to watch. And then she was explaining how she'd tried all evening to find us and had "made so many calls." Finally she'd gone to a place where Americans were clearing up the oil spill. She'd given one of them Scotty's travel pouch—thinking, because both this man and Scotty worked for the federal government, the man would know how to find us.

"How?" I asked. How had she found Scotty's purse? "And where?" I couldn't stop crying.

"I listened to what you told the driver," she said. "I had him take me to your stop. Otherwise, it would have been stolen." And now—in a city of more than one million locals and thousands of tourists—she "just happened" to be looking out her market window?

The girl suggested we go immediately to where the American would be working. She also asked us to count the money. "It will all be there," I heard her say, as I remembered the doubts I'd earlier expressed regarding integrity. "Scotty, they don't think like we do," I'd said. No, I wasn't prejudiced, I'd added. I just knew what I knew—only I didn't. I hadn't known a thing about these people—nor had I known my heart harbored such prejudice.

Within minutes of having met Jacqueline, Scotty and I both hugged her while shoppers exclaimed, "Incredible!" That much money lost? Not even in the U.S., they were saying, had they heard about that kind of money being returned. A cabby born in Brooklyn declared it was a miracle. And the handsome, black American with the back-home grin and Scotty's wallet? He was waiting. And the cash? Every penny there.

After we'd returned with a reward for the young clerk, Scotty and I were walking hand-in-hand toward our hotel, and I was telling him how sorry I was for the nagging I'd done earlier. "But—" I began.

"But do I think God had anything to do with this?" Scotty smiled.

"Yes," I said.

He nodded.

"And that you'll get a promotion?" I asked.

"Yes," he said, "I believe." He took my hand. "But, Babe, did *you* notice what street her shop was on?"

I hadn't.

"It's called 'calle del Cristo.'" He pulled a map from his pocket. "Cristo Street . . . Christ," he said.

I was crying.

"And the chapel we visited?" He smiled again. "Built to commemorate a miracle."

"A miracle," I breathed—and for us there had been three. Our money had been returned, and Scotty's faith in God—and mine in people—had been renewed.

We had experienced our own miracle . . . on Cristo Street.

26

Gray Hairs

The glory of young men is their strength, gray hair the splendor of the old.

Proverbs 20:29

My Seattle sister, visiting me in Northern Virginia, had been telling me for some time she could color my hair if I wanted her to.

"I don't want you to," I said.

"I've been doing mine for years."

I knew that; what I didn't know was just what color it had originally been, I told her.

"Not funny," she said. "And, seriously, yours *could* be so pretty, and you *would* look so much younger—"

"I tried it; I didn't like it; the last person who fiddled with it turned it burgundy and purple—and, before that, something resembling lime. Not a good shade on me," I said. I tossed her a smile I almost meant, thought how it isn't good to have rifts between ourselves and other family members, suggested it would be a good idea if she remembered the same. Could we change the subject and forget changing me? She was as bad as my youngest daughter, always "suggesting" what it was I "could" wear.

Okay, if I wouldn't let her color my hair—or pick out a different outfit—how about breakfast at McDonald's, and then we'd do the mall?

I wanted to tell her I didn't do malls either. The last time she'd visited, we'd spent nine hours there, and we'd only covered half of the place, and I'd made countless trips to *my* car with *her* packages. "McDonald's sounds great," I said. At least I'd get decent coffee there for only twenty-five cents. "Senior coffee" they called it, a reward for having made it to over fifty—which was and still is fine with me.

We'd barely gotten to the counter when a teen smiled first at me and then directly at my sister. "Can I help you?" he asked her and then me.

I already knew I wanted a breakfast burrito; my sister said she'd have the same. I also wanted coffee.

"Me, too," my sister said—and I remembered she'd always said "Me, too!" to Santa and when Grandma had asked me what I wanted for lunch. This morning, my sister also wanted cream and sugar.

The boy grinned, but my sister wasn't looking at him. She was stirring her purse and insisting this would be her treat. Her mind more on shopping than anything else, she was frantically yanking both lists and bills from her billfold—when the teenager turned to give our order to an equally youthful cook.

"Burritos!" he shouted. "And two senior coffees," he said.

Suddenly, shopping lists and dollar bills took a backseat, as my sister whipped her red-haired head up and around and pinned the young man with a look.

"Who are you calling a *senior?*" she whooped.

The startled boy stared back at my sister. "Well," he said, shuffling like a politician. "Anyone older than me?"

I wanted to tell him he should run for governor, but I couldn't. I was laughing. While I had to admit she looked great, my sister's belief in Madison Avenue's "Fountain of Youth" hadn't entirely done it for her—and she most definitely wouldn't be doing it for me. "We're 'Gray Hairs,'" I said, using a term my youngest had laughingly attached to my husband and me. "The splendor of the old—which is perfectly fine with me," I added, as we found ourselves a clean table. "And so is the 'senior coffee,'" I said—while my sister, though not yet fully recovered—laughed.

Old age, senior, gray hair, retiree, and over the hill. Why do we continue to fight this special season? God had a plan from the very beginning; he said all our hairs are numbered. I believe he meant not just the burgundy and blue hairs—but the silver and white ones, too.

Succumb to the "Fountain of Youth" supposition? Pluck or color the graying hairs on my own head and look back wishing and thinking, *If only I could be young again?*

No way! Not me.

Part 4

How?

Trust in the Lord with all your heart and lean not on your own understanding; in all your ways acknowledge him, and he will make your paths straight.

Proverbs 3:5–6

27

Buried Alive in Bismarck

How can we sing the songs of the LORD while in a foreign land?

Psalm 137:4

Scotty's work would be moving us again, but this time we were going west. West was good; I'd longed for this for several years. West meant mountains and tall trees. It might even mean lakes with white sand and picnics without mosquitos and hiking to where an entire valley could be seen.

West, however, for this move meant North Dakota. A state I'd never been to. We'd traveled in and through South Dakota many times—had never grown weary of staring at Mount Rushmore, thought the Passion Play in Spearfish was the best. We'd even spent several gorgeous nights in cabins up the canyon, and I'd been treated to my first buffalo burger in a small café in Custer.

And then there was Montana. Home in my heart, the place where snow could be seen on mountains in August and where the valleys were wide and green and people waved when they drove by.

"But *North* Dakota?" a friend had asked. Just the week before, she'd heard Chuck Swindoll say something like, "There are few things as lonely as going through a test and having no friend to call." Was this going to be another test? Had I ever been there?

"No, I haven't been there," I said, but it was west, so I was looking forward to whatever this move might be.

I looked forward only until we hit the border on the eastern edge of Fargo. I didn't tell Scotty, however, that I was beginning to feel this funny feeling inside. I didn't say, "This doesn't look like anything I imagined." I didn't shout, "You turn this truck around!" Instead, I told myself that Bismarck was the capitol and that it wouldn't look anything like the countryside I'd seen so far. I knew for certain there'd be a river; that much I'd learned from my Rand McNally. The Missouri, if I remembered correctly, which would be good enough for me. Maybe there would be swimming. If not, fishing would do. Maybe we'd find a home on its banks, and then we'd put a dock in, and the grandkids would come there to spend their summers with us. And no doubt there would also be deer.

Thirty miles east of Bismarck, I began to smell something fishy. What was it Moses had said? "If your Spirit doesn't go with me, don't send me up there"? The land we'd traveled was flatter than the back of my hand. "Where are all the mountains?" I finally managed to peep.

For several minutes, Scotty said nothing.

"Where are all the mountains?" I repeated—as I watched my husband wrestle with what looked like a sheepish grin.

"In Montana, Babe," was all that he said—but I completely lost it.

"In *Montana?*" He wasn't kidding? We wouldn't have any mountains to look at? It was going to be flatter than a frying pan?

Scotty nodded.

"But you said—"

"That we were going west, Babe," he said. "I didn't say it would look exactly like—"

He may have said more, but I'd made up my mind I would *not* listen. I'd listened to too many of his stories already—stories about adventure, tall tales about romance. Those fables were the reason I'd agreed to go along with four relocations already—which didn't begin to count the "in-betweens." No, I wasn't going to listen anymore. I'd make the best of what was coming, but I would not be glad.

In Bismarck, we'd only just unloaded all our trailer belongings inside a narrow room in yet another strange motel, when Scotty announced he'd have to travel. Before I'd even discovered where his local office would be, he wasn't going to be there. He would be on the road, while I would wait in a room with a view of the parking lot and a sign pointing the way to Minot. That same week, I was given a taste of North Dakota snow. Friends "just happened" to stop over for a night at the same motel, which meant I had someone to talk to over breakfast. But even their telling me "God has a plan for your life" hadn't helped. I wanted out, and I wanted out *now.*

"There are so many beautiful things in this world," I wrote a friend, "but you can't see any of them from here." I'd had enough moves, done enough adjusting. In Bismarck—a place that reminded me of a pair of stout boots—a person couldn't even get a cup of Starbucks coffee! And a Nordstom's store? The closest one could be found *where?* Worse, the one night I thought I'd actu-

157

ally enjoy watching TV, someone decided to preempt Martha Stewart with high school basketball!

The afternoon I discovered I couldn't even get a latte without driving clear across town, I thought my world had come to an end—until Cheryl called. I hadn't yet met her, but our husbands would be working together; she knew most of the women whose husbands occupied offices in my husband's building. Would I like to meet for coffee somewhere? Would I like to meet some of the other wives?

When a new wife hits town and she's missing her "real friends" and picturing herself anywhere but here, the words "Would you like to meet?" are right up there with angels singing. Would I like to meet other wives, have coffee, go to lunch, come to Cheryl's house?

"All of the above!" I sang. I could be ready in less time than it would take for her to come and get me. I would be getting out of this dismal motel, seeing a real house, drinking real coffee, sharing with women who would be nothing like the daytime television personalities with no personalities at all!

"You needed this," Cheryl said, pouring me a cup of home-brewed coffee.

And she was right; I did.

Two weeks later, when I hit a low again, Cheryl pointed out that I also needed my "stuff." Nearly everything we owned—including pictures of the grandkids, and the dolls I collected, and teapots, and cups—and even dried weeds—still took up space in a warehouse rented for storage. We wouldn't be moving into a real home for at least five or maybe six weeks.

Cheryl kept me from losing my mind. Once we'd moved into our "permanent" house, she continued to be the friend I needed. She also introduced me to other friends, and before long I had joined a Bible study. In that Bible study, I met women who invited me to walk with them in the morning, women who lived for antique hunts, women who understood it wasn't easy being a woman sometimes.

The day winter put its roots down deep, friends became even more important. I still loathed Bismarck, North Dakota—not easy to love a place when the temperature has dropped to 80 below with the wind chill and you're being warned not even to go to your own mailbox. Not easy when the winds pick up and a tree comes down on your home. Not easy in the summer, either, when there are layers upon layers of grasshoppers that crunch when you walk on your walk and who plaster themselves all over the brick of your house and across the entire width of the garage door.

But I liked my friends; I needed them; they were what I looked forward to when I'd get up each morning. When you've grown up with city delights, lakes, mountains, and trees, you begin to think you'll never again know joy in a place like North Dakota. You think that *only* before you've been invited for a cappuccino at a filling station.

Yes, a filling station. "Cappuccino Tuesday" is what we decided to dub it. On Tuesdays, half a dozen of us met at the Cenex. Not just for cappuccino but for silliness and laughter. Not just because we needed to get out of the house but to offer moral support. I'd think I couldn't deal with another North Dakota winter day, and a friend would call to remind me it was Tuesday.

I'd tell Scotty—via the telephone—that I thought I was going to go crazy, but then a friend would knock at the door, tell me she had her car warmed up, and I was to come quick and see the sunset. I'd begin to talk about renting my own apartment in Montana somewhere, and one of the wives would call to say she was going to the Wal-Mart Store and did I want to ride along. Not long after we moved in, someone opened an A & W, and several of us began to meet there for lunch and laughter.

You think this doesn't sound like fun? When I lived in cities like Albuquerque and Seattle, I'll admit it didn't sound like fun to me. But in Bismarck I learned that fun has everything to do with friendship, that with friends you can enjoy doing hamburgers at Burger King or dinners on the Missouri River—so long as you all stick together.

Friendships formed by women who've endured a long, cold winter are the friendships you do not forget. It doesn't matter that we've moved twice since my North Dakota experience—where at first it appeared to me that nothing good could grow—because I'd come away with something that would last more than just a season. I'd learned about the joy of simple things, about the goodness there can be in people, that caring can be imparted by strangers who know how to hear. I'd learned these things in a place where Bible studies and homemade fun and cookies and even old tunes on a player piano could be the highlight of a woman's day. And though we spent just two years in Bismarck—and some days I'll admit I felt as if it had been not just two but twenty—I came away knowing that while it may appear you and I have little in common, we each bring a unique self to any setting, and there can be a growing.

I came away knowing I hadn't been buried but blessed.

28

The Hairs on My Head Are Numbered?

"Indeed, the very hairs of your head are all numbered. Don't be afraid; you are worth more than many sparrows."

Luke 12:7

For women who have frequently moved because of their husband's work or even their own, the search for a stylist is right up there with trusting a dentist. My worst fear, actually. Cleaning teeth, drilling, fixing cavities? *Nothing* compared to the trauma some of us suffer when the stranger with the scissors begins to size up the shape of our face and the way we hold our head *and* tries to imagine how we might look with "a little something new."

I know this from experience. We've relocated fifteen times in twenty-six years—if you count the apartments, motels, and our daughter's basement between homes.

Not until our most recent move did I find someone the first time around. Prior to that, it was just one disaster after another, followed by tears, followed by my threatening not only to perm but to cut my own hair!

"You know the difference between a good and a bad haircut, don't you?" Scotty would delight in asking. "About two weeks," he'd say.

I've never laughed at this too-close-to-home joke, although I'll admit my husband does have a sense of humor. I know he's even walked through some pretty bad cuts, himself. But unlike me, he simply waits it out, tries again. Wears a hat.

But it's not *his* haircuts I'm recalling; I'm remembering mine. I'm also remembering a particular stylist—and that even though I cried for days, I also learned in North Dakota that God had not only *numbered* my hairs but that he had his eye on my head, and he cared about my looking good.

I'd asked around; I always do. I notice a woman on the street or in a restaurant, think she doesn't look half bad, walk over and ask, "Who cuts your hair?", then call whatever stylist she's suggested. In Bismarck, however, the same girl who'd done wonders with a woman checking groceries at the store did her worst for me. I knew for a fact that this cut was going to take longer than the "predicted" weeks.

"This *always* happens!" I'd shrieked, back home and asking to borrow one of Scotty's caps. "And no I will *not* go out anywhere," I'd told him—except to church. I needed church; I needed the fellowship; maybe the singing and the worship would make me forget.

The following Sunday morning, we visited a congregation near our motel and received a warming welcome from kind faces, smiling faces, people who shook our hands. One young woman in particular said how very glad she was to see us there. We were to tell her if we needed anything at all.

The following day—even though I'd threatened not to leave the house—I needed groceries and postage stamps. I'd also decided I would treat myself to a lunch. I'd write my lists and figure out what to do with myself while I waited to be moved to yet another place. I'd also figure out what to do with my hair.

"This isn't a simple matter, Lord," I said, bowing my head over my salad, and instead of asking a blessing on the food, begging him to answer. Where would I go now? I'd asked the few women I'd met so far, but all of them went to the girl I would not go to again. They'd suggested I give her another chance, but I told them I had my limits. "So, please, Father," I prayed. "Couldn't you just show me who it is I need to see?"

Between the salad and the sherbet, a thought came. "Go across the street," it seemed to say.

Across the street? I glanced out through the café window, but all I could see was a cell phone shop, a cleaners, and a place where they sold submarines. Sandwiches, that is. "You want me to go to—?"

Again the thought came to cross the street. In fact, this time the "thought" was so strong, I almost forgot to pay the check. He knew someone there? Someone who might help? Someone who could undo what had already been done to me?

Across the street, I discovered a storefront I couldn't have seen from the restaurant window. Across the street and just around the corner a bit from the cell phone store, I discovered one of those salons where all the cuts are only eleven dollars. One of those styling salons where I'd been told they completely butcher your hair.

You want me to go in there? I waited for another better thought, but nothing came.

Meanwhile, I noted the place was nearly filled with clients wrapped in capes and happily chatting with women who actually looked like they knew what they were doing. Maybe if I watched a little while, I could pick out the one person who'd know what to do with me. Maybe if I waited in one of the chairs and pretended to be reading—

"Hi!" I heard, as a young woman stepped up beside me. From out of thin air she'd appeared; she'd obviously been in the back room. I wouldn't turn around; I'd pretend I hadn't heard. If all of these other customers were happy, then I wanted one of the stylists styling *their* hair. I didn't want some woman who'd been spending her time in some storage room. If she was any good at all, wouldn't she have been out here?

I turned around to say "Hi" back—and also to tell her I guessed I'd changed my mind—when I realized she looked familiar. "I . . ." I said. "I . . ." I said again. I knew I should smile and saw that she was smiling. "I was thinking of getting my hair cut again," I said, "but now I'm not sure."

She nodded.

"I have some pictures . . ." My stomach had gone into the position it always assumes when someone with the scissors begins to look at me. "I'm looking at the time," I said, glancing at the clock. Plenty of time, actually. I turned to look again at the smiling stylist. "But you look familiar!" I blurted, feeling foolish and wishing I had never come through her door.

"You visited our church," she said. "I was yesterday's greeter."

"Yes!" She'd greeted us! She'd been the one who'd smiled as a friend might, the one who'd said how glad she was that we'd come to visit. She'd been the one who'd shown us where the coffee would be served, where we could hang our coats, where to sit to better enjoy the music.

"But if you don't have the time today," she was saying, "we can set up an appointment."

"I *have* the time," I said, smiling, too, and thinking how good a smile could feel. I had lots of time. Time to get my hair styled, time to visit, time to think how only minutes before I hadn't known where I would be going. Time to remember that I'd asked, "Father, please give me a sign." Time to recall he'd done such a thing for Gideon, and I didn't ask often, but this morning I'd needed him to give one also to me.

"I have the time," I said again, slipping out of my coat, "and I need—"

"To have something done with your hair," she said, moving around first to my right and then my left, studying the shape of my face and the condition of my current "style."

"We'll take care of you," she said, her voice reassuring as she nodded toward the station that was hers. "We'll take good care of you," she said this time.

And she did. And so had God. And that day I went home not in tears but via the round-about route that included a visit to my husband's office. I had something not only to tell but to show. God had done a perfect work; he'd not only numbered the hairs on my head, but he'd seen to it that they were properly trimmed.

"Even to your old age and gray hairs I am he, I am he who will sustain you. I have made you and I will carry you; I will sustain you and I will rescue you" (Isa. 46:4).

Think God doesn't care about the things that are important to us?

Think again.

29

The Tornado
and the Time-Out

He stilled the storm to a whisper.

Psalm 107:29a

We hadn't fully moved into our house in Bismarck, North Dakota, when I began to hear about the disturbing tornadoes that almost never materialized—but that in some parts of the state, they frequently experienced the real thing. So, the night Scotty was out of town and I heard the sirens begin? I ran to the window—which was the first thing I'd been told *not* to do; I grabbed the cat and squeezed him so tight it's a wonder he's still with us. Then—after several circles around both the inside and the outside of my house and all the while watching the blackened western horizon—I called the neighbor next door.

I hadn't known these people all that long, but I did know they knew how to be good neighbors. During our first Dakota snowstorm, the man who lived there had bundled in protective clothing, gotten out his snow-blower, *and* cleared our three-car driveway and the walks. No one had even said a word to him about coming to help; he'd just done it, because he and his wife had noticed my husband was again out of town. In those days, I think it was easier to notice the handful of days he was *home*. At any rate, I knew the neighbor was a neighbor, so I called.

"I've never lived where there are tornadoes! What's going to happen?" I said, sounding a little more shrill than I meant to and dumping the cat on the floor. "What should I do? Get under the bed? Stand inside an interior doorway?"

"Where are you now?" my neighbor asked.

"In front of the dining room window," I said. I needed to see what the rest of the town was doing.

"No windows," he said. "Go down to the basement; you need to go now."

I didn't want to go to the basement; I don't like basements. "But there are only three windows down there," I said.

"That's why," he said. "No windows. Get out of the dining room; turn off the radio—and hang up the phone."

I couldn't be on the phone? If I hung up, I'd have only the cat.

"We'd tell you to come over here," he said, "but you really need to get downstairs. My kids are already in our basement."

"The basement," I said, wishing he'd tell me it was okay for me to run from our house to his. Wishing I was there already. Wishing my husband didn't have to travel out of state when a tornado was coming to town.

Reluctantly hanging up the receiver, I grabbed my cat and began to run. I could see the sky had grown dark, and the siren hadn't stopped, and every one of our trees had begun to bow down, and outside it sounded as if a locomotive was coming through the neighborhood.

In the basement, I found the corner my neighbor had suggested. The one with no windows, away from the lights and the doors. And with my cat on my lap, I sat. My neighbor had suggested—and even Scotty had mentioned before he'd packed—that I might want to have a portable, battery-operated radio downstairs, but I'd forgotten, so I wouldn't have any way of knowing when the danger had passed—except that our neighbor had said he would call. That part I remembered. He'd said, "When it's safe to come out of the basement, we will let you know."

Thirty minutes later, I hadn't yet heard the telephone. With our basement walls as thick as they were and with no windows to see through and no radio announcing "All is well," I had no idea what was going on outside.

An hour later, I continued to wait. Now I was really frightened. What if the tornado had come through our neighborhood, struck our neighbor's house, missed ours—and not only would no one call, but no one would be living? I glanced at my wrist to see if maybe my watch had stopped, and then I turned to my cat. "Do you understand that we might be in terrible danger?" I said. Had he heard anything with those cat ears of his? Didn't animals pick up things a human could not? Why hadn't I thought to bring a book?

Two hours later, I'd had it with the waiting. Yes, I'd finally given up and become quiet—which was something I'd been avoiding for days. Still, I couldn't stay alone in an ugly basement another minute. I needed to see if the neighbor's house was standing. I needed to know where the storm was. Maybe it had gone around our town.

Upstairs, I discovered an evening full of sunlight and a sky that had turned copper and blue—but there was no one on the streets and no children in any yard.

Going for the phone, I immediately dialed my neighbor's number—and within seconds heard not only his wife in the background but his children, the dog, *and* the television.

"The *storm?*" I croaked. "I thought . . . that you were going to," I began—and realized my neighbor had grown strangely silent. We'd already discovered he was a quiet man by nature, but after his initial "Hello," he usually said a little something before he turned the conversation over to his spouse.

I glanced at my cat chasing dust balls in the light of the sun. "Didn't you say you would call?" A television? They'd been watching my favorite television program, while *I'd* been sitting in that basement for who knew how long?

"I forgot," I heard my neighbor say.

"You forgot—?"

"To call," he said. "I'm sorry."

He was sorry? I'd hunkered down on a wooden step stool with a cat in the dark forever? I'd not only waited for what I hoped would be good news, but I'd waited thinking a tornado might take the roof off the top of my home? And I'd done all that waiting alone—for nothing? He hadn't remembered promising he would call? I couldn't see him, of course, but I could imagine a shrug. I was overreacting, and he probably knew it. Truth was, I knew it, too.

"Oh . . . well . . . that's okay," I said—but as I hung up the receiver, I began to look around at my surroundings, began to think of the thoughts I'd thought while waiting—and I knew it was more than okay. Prior to the

169

warning, I'd been fretting. I'd wrestled with anger, thought it was high time my husband put an end to his travel, wondered if this was the right house, thought that maybe—if we'd been allowed a little more time— we could have come up with something better. I'd turned my stomach into a tight knot but not over the storm warning at all. I'd done so simply because I'd started thinking too far into my future, and the thinking hadn't been good. I'd skipped my quiet prayer time for several mornings, because I'd been bent on stewing instead.

But then my neighbor had said he'd call, and I'd gone down to that basement. And sitting there, I'd begun not just to pray for my safety and the safety of our home, but I'd prayed for each of my neighbors. Next, I'd talked to the Lord about some other people. Friends, colleagues, a couple much too close to divorcing. I'd considered my blessings, decided it really wasn't so terrible to have a husband who traveled. The bottom line was that he came home. Not only that, he came home looking forward to home. He came home ready to take me out for dinner, even though he'd been eating every one of his meals in one hotel after another. He came home asking what *I'd* like to do. If what I'd like was antique shopping, he'd go with me. If I wanted to take a drive clear across the state, he'd say, "Great!"

And our home? Actually, though there were days when I wondered if it was really what I wanted or even needed, I had a home. That was the point, really, that I had one. Hadn't I just heard again from a friend who lived where there'd been a succession of floods and her husband still had no work? Hadn't she recently written that they would be forced to find emergency housing? Hadn't a missionary acquaintance written to say how very grateful she was, after having suffered through not just one but several earthquakes, that they'd been issued makeshift lodging?

For two hours in that basement, I'd prayed, and God had stilled the storm that had been raging for a very long time—a storm that had been growing inside me.

The following morning, my neighbor's wife met me at the mailbox. "I'm so sorry," she said, "that he forgot to call you. If I'd known—"

I shook my head and smiled. "No," I said, "don't be sorry. I needed that."

My neighbor's expression made it clear she thought I was just trying to be polite. "You needed two hours alone in your *basement?*"

I laughed. "Yes," I said. "Actually, I did." I glanced back at my house again, wondered how it was that I could have thought it was something far less than what I'd hoped it would be.

"Well, there's no excuse—"

"No," I said, "no excuse." None for the complaints I'd been voicing over the past several weeks, and none for the way I'd been acting. I smiled. "He forgot," I said . . . "and I needed a time-out."

Later that afternoon as I listened to the news, I heard the report that the tornado had never even touched down in Bismarck. But, for me, something truly significant had happened. I'd been given two hours to focus on God and the many ways he had been blessing me.

30

We Can't All
Live Upstream

He who despises his neighbor sins, but blessed is he who is kind to the needy.

Proverbs 14:21

Devastating floods had covered much of North Dakota. Plans had been suggested for diverting the water onto farmland above where the worst damage had been done but, according to reports, people who hadn't been caught by the fury of the rivers weren't interested in hearing how they could help. They were doing just fine, thank you, several had said via the local news. And about all that water on the lower half of the state? Someone else's problem, not theirs; they didn't want to hear about this business anymore.

At first, I blamed the belligerence and harsh words on the men alone. They were North Dakotans, I said.

They'd grown up during hard times and in hard places, and they just didn't care about people all that much anymore. That's what I thought, that is, before I walked into a ladies' room in a hotel after a statewide meeting . . . and overheard the "ladies" talking amongst themselves.

"If they think *we're* going to take their water," one woman was practically shouting, "they have another think coming." They were doing just fine up where they lived, and the people in the south could just take care of themselves.

Only they couldn't, I wanted to say. Instead, I brushed my windblown hair and continued to listen.

"Yeah," another farm wife was saying now. "They were talkin' to us about that stuff, too, and we told them they could forget it." She and her husband had both decided they weren't going to let anyone come in and tell *them* what to do. Divert all that water on their good land and create those wetlands the government was so excited about? "Nope," the wife said then. "We told *them*."

I understood their reluctance to deal with anyone representing a government agency; they hadn't been happy—and some of them with good reason—about lots of "government things" that had happened in their state years ago and even this year. But not to care about a neighbor?

"And they're not neighbors, either," a third woman huffed as she powdered her face. "City people—or they might as well be," she said. "Livin' that close to Fargo."

Together, the women laughed.

City people? I didn't read the papers often, but I read them enough to know we weren't talking about city dwellers. The folks who were currently in trouble—with the rivers and that enormous lake up north taking over their land—were farmers. Farmers exactly like the ones in the northern part of the state. The only difference? The people downstream had suffered from a flood that would deal with them for years, a flood they'd been able to do nothing about.

Later that evening as we drove back home, I began to relate to Scotty what I'd overheard. "It makes me so sad," I said. "And not just that they don't care about helping out . . . but because I'd expected more from women."

"Compassion," Scotty said.

I nodded.

"Babe, they're people, flesh and blood. It's human nature for them to respond the way they did."

Human nature? I didn't want to believe that. I didn't want to think that people in the same boat—some with and others without water—could turn their backs when such a need came. On the other hand, what was it I'd heard a Christian friend say just the week before? "I'm sorry about all of that famine, but we have our own to think about." We'd been discussing a news report about women and children starving to death on week-long walks, walks they'd hoped would get them to where relief volunteers might offer them food.

"It makes me sad," I said now.

Scotty nodded. "But remember the other night when we mentioned the man up the street battling cancer and maybe all the neighbors could help by mowing his lawn—and with whatever else he needed?" He'd already started doing odd jobs for this man and for his wife, whenever they would let him.

I remembered. Our next-door neighbor had stared at us like we were crazy, said something about her own yard and that she and her husband had enough to do. I also remembered occasionally driving by the home of an elderly woman sitting out on her porch, and I'd wonder if she lived alone, whether her children ever came if she had some. I'd wonder if she might like a ride, might like to have lunch in town—but I never once asked. No, she didn't exactly live next door, but wasn't she also my neighbor? Hadn't I seen it written that one meaning of the word *neighbor* is "a fellow man (or woman)"?

I remember a winter when Scotty's work took him to one of the southern states and left me behind in the north. He hadn't been out of town twenty-four hours when the worst snowfall of the year hit. It took me three days to dig a path to the main road. An elderly widow lived across the road; it took her three days to dig out as well. Slowly she'd shovel and sweep, give me a wave, head for the house to rest, come back out, and try again. And the man who lived on the other side of our place, a man who owned a John Deere tractor? He cleared just one drive, his own.

Later, I told my widow friend that we didn't want to be too hard on this man. Maybe he just wasn't able to afford the fuel it might have taken to get us *all* out to the road. Maybe it never occurred to him we'd be happy to pay. Not only that, the man worked in the city and commuted an hour or more. Maybe his excuse was fatigue. Somehow, though, all my wondering didn't make me feel all that much better about a man who could watch an elderly widow shovel snow.

Today, with cities so crowded and felt distance between people who were once friends and neighbors, we don't seem to care much about the others anymore. We fence our spaces, employ answering machines, and keep our shades drawn. The night I listened to the farm wives in the ladies' room, I realized this new attitude has begun to make its way out to where life is rural. Even people who work with their hands, people with roots that go back to working shoulder-to-shoulder to settle families in a harsh land, seem to have little time for goodwill.

I remember, as a city kid, visiting a cousin's farm in Washington State and how very much I learned there. It helped that we could listen in on party lines, but even as a child, I could see that folks on farms didn't just talk a good game. Instead, they rolled up their sleeves when neighbors needed to get a crop in. When cows calved, fellow farmers came, and when it was Sunday, hired hands and family gathered around chicken dinners that welcomed strangers as well.

Before he died, the husband of the widow in our old neighborhood used to say, "If you want a good neighbor, you have to be a good neighbor." This morning, I ask myself if I'm good. To tell you the truth, I don't remember the last time I did anything really significant for anyone—unless you want to count the time I took in the widow's mail. No, I can't actually call that commendable. I did feed her cat once, but I didn't exactly put myself out.

Several months ago, I went shopping for a baby gift for one of the women in my husband's office. I knew her name and knew where she'd registered, but when I entered the baby department of a store unfamiliar to me, I discovered there were two women expecting babies, women with exactly the same name. The only way I'd be able to know for certain I was buying what my husband's secretary needed was to call.

"I need to call my husband," I said. "He'll know her address, and then I'll be able to buy the right thing."

"Long distance," a female clerk said, as she continued to fold bags and sort out a stack of baby clothes.

"Long distance?"

She nodded.

"I don't have a calling card," I said then, "and I don't think my husband's employer will appreciate my calling him collect." I tried to smile, wondered if just maybe this department store had a line I could use that would connect me direct.

The woman shook her head. "No," she'd said, when one of the tallest men I've ever seen stepped up to the counter next to me. He was holding a telephone receiver *and* a calling card. "Use my card." He nodded. "Please," he said, with the most wonderful and unfamiliar accent.

"Oh, I couldn't do that," I told him. "I just thought—"

The man smiled. "We were put on this earth to help each other," he said, placing the plastic card in the palm of my hand.

It took no more than a couple of minutes for me to call my husband and to find out which woman's baby I would be buying for. It will take me a lifetime to consider what that man offered that day. "I'm from Sierra Leone," he said, after I'd made my call. "It's not safe for me to go home, but I use these cards to make certain my family is well." This man had walked through multiplied pain and abuse unlike anything anyone in my own country could imagine. And, doing so, he'd become what the dictionary—and God's Word—describes as a real neighbor.

But in that ladies' room with the farm wives telling one another how they would not lift a finger for those people in the south? According to what Scotty had said weeks before, those women—along with their husbands—had decided not to be neighbors.

I had wanted to tell them this wasn't about wetlands or an overabundance of water. I had wanted to say, "We are humans, but we were created to be so much more." I had wanted to remind them that the day could come when they might also need another to come alongside. But then I considered someone else who also needed to be reminded—on a daily basis—to be a neighbor.

We can't all live upstream, I said just to me.

31

Casting Blame

"But they all alike began to make excuses."

Luke 14:18a

Have you ever told someone you'd do something you didn't really want to do? Agreed to accept an office or to teach in the nursery? Blamed your regrets on a family member? Made a dozen excuses and wished you'd kept your lips zipped instead? I have. Many times, too many times—and now here I was in the middle of one of those times again.

I'd agreed to be the new treasurer for a local Christian women's club; I'd agreed even though I had writing assignments and deadlines—not to mention a house to completely redo. Scotty had gone out of town with his work; I'd wanted to go out of town with mine. Instead, I'd agreed to sit at a table to sell admission tickets; I was to make sure the money came out right and that our speakers were paid. I'd also agreed to deliver a suitcase full of the books our Book Chairman would be selling; these sales were extremely important, since we would be sending all the proceeds to missionaries all over the world.

"*Please* don't leave those books sitting in your garage," our Book Chairman had said when she'd given them to me.

Forget? Me? The firstborn perfectionist? I laughed.

Now, I'd arrived early, which hadn't been easy. With my husband away, there'd been no one but me to haul out the garbage, feed the cat, *and* straighten up. To add to my time crunch, I'd given a ride to a woman who'd needed one. I'd also agreed to open my home for a Bible study after the larger meeting adjourned. I'd outdone myself, I told myself—feeling more than a little puffed-up about all I'd agreed to do. Puffed-up, that is, until our Book Chairman walked into the room—looking for her books.

"Books?" I glanced left, then right, and behind me. I *couldn't* have forgotten; I'd written myself a note. I never forgot things like this. "The *books?*" I croaked—"Are at my house, but—"

It took our Book Chairman less than thirty seconds to traverse the noisy room to where she could plant herself squarely in front of me.

"Where *are* they?" she was asking. "I need them; I can't sell them if they're not here." She sounded breathless; she also sounded like a woman about to ask me where I'd left my head.

"I'll *get* them," I snapped back over my shoulder, as I abandoned my chair and the tickets and the people standing in line to give their cash to me. Why hadn't she called? *How difficult would that have been?* She could have reminded me, for heaven's sake! I slammed my hip against the revolving exit door.

We held our meetings north of town; I lived all the way south. *God, please,* I prayed, pulling into heavy traffic. *Please make the traffic lights stay green for me.* I couldn't afford to panic. I knew from experience that panic attacks were not a good mix in a situation like this. No matter what, I would not scream.

Shifting first to the left lane and then right, I pictured my husband packing his luggage. Hadn't he promised he'd put those books in my car? *If he hadn't forgotten . . .* How could I be expected to remember everything? Why couldn't a man do what he'd said he would do? *How difficult would that have been?*

I signaled for another left turn, pretending not to notice the light had changed. "If the woman had just called to remind me," I said. *If she'd come earlier like the rest of us, then wouldn't I have remembered in time?* But no, she hadn't gotten there until fifteen minutes before we were supposed to meet, and now look what trouble she'd caused for me. Those books were her responsibility; why had she let me take them to my house in the first place? I wondered how National Headquarters would feel about her doing a thing like that.

On the other hand, she'd done so, I reminded myself, because I'd asked to see them, and because she was doing me a favor. Still, she'd played a part in this current dilemma, and I had a right to be mad. *I wonder how she'd like to be driving this fast through this mess!*

Picking up speed and passing a fast-food drive-thru with a stream of traffic trying to exit a parking lot, I signaled again and had just darted in front of a slower driver when I caught The Law Enforcement Center out of the corner of my eye—and I braked. *Slow down,* I breathed. *Father, don't let me get a ticket!* Did God answer prayers from speeders? Maybe not—but a person could hope.

I glared at a second slow-moving vehicle; glanced at my watch; tried relaxing. Actually, I was making pretty good time. *If I hadn't given Jan a ride this morning. . . .* Because she's legally blind, I often drove her to where she needed to be; she certainly couldn't be expected to get there on her own. But what did the others have that was so all-fired important? Why hadn't someone else volunteered? Did they not see that I was more than a little busy? It was getting so I had to do everything!

Five blocks from home, I'd only just rounded the corner, when I spotted what I hadn't anticipated. At least one dozen members of a road crew, most of them standing around—but two of them putting up a barricade?

"No!" I had no time for detours; why did they always have to be working where people needed to be driving? Praying they wouldn't stop me, I whipped my wheels to a tight right around the end of the obstruction. I wouldn't look back at the startled men; they might be taking down my number; I wouldn't let myself see them do that.

To my amazement, no one tried to stop me or even seemed to care. Within minutes, I'd wheeled into my driveway, hit the automatic opener, and found the missing case. Then it was a simple matter to just fling it into the car and to start back along the way I had gone. I'd pulled this "mission" off in record time!

"Next month, though," I said to my rearview mirror, "they can just find someone else to take care of that table." I was tired of working with women who never followed through; women were the pits. You couldn't rely on any of them; they had no sense of what it meant to be responsible.

Dashing down the hall of the hotel between circles of chatter and wondering just how much these dumb books weighed, I could hear the speaker winding up—and I'd sighed a breath of relief near the door—when I spotted a new friend, one from a neighboring town. She was standing alone, appearing puzzled and a little bit shy and looking for a place to sit. But why? She'd never come to one of these meetings before—and now she was waving at *me?*

"Hi," I sang. "What a nice surprise."

"Surprise?" My new friend frowned. "Actually," she said, "I was . . . well . . . getting worried."

Worried?

She looked flushed; had something happened? The case of books at my hip, I nodded toward the Book Chairman's table to indicate I needed to keep going. "Worried?" I said back over my shoulder and shifting the box of books again.

"Well . . . I thought maybe you'd forgotten," she said.

"Forgotten?" This time I turned all the way around and stared. "Forgot?" I started to utter again—when I glanced at the date on my watch and remembered. *I'd* invited her; *I* was the one who'd suggested she might like to join us—but I'd forgotten. "I didn't . . . couldn't," I said—but I had. This time, I couldn't blame my husband; I couldn't blame our Book Chairman; I couldn't blame the road crew, the traffic, my cat, or Jan.

Dropping the bulky books on a shaky wooden table, I looked directly at the Chairman who looked relieved, and then I looked directly at my friend. "I did," I said, knowing I was the one who'd flushed this time. "I forgot," I added—finally and correctly casting blame.

32

How to Destroy
a Friendship
and a Bible Study

Therefore each of you must put off falsehood and speak
truthfully to his neighbor, for we are all members of one
body.

Ephesians 4:25

Have you ever been invited to someone's home, a luncheon, whatever—and you didn't want to go there—but
you also didn't want to say no and make yourself look
bad or risk upsetting a friend or neighbor?

I have. I'm guessing maybe we *all* have. We receive
the invitation; we place it on the refrigerator—or in a
drawer somewhere. If it's in the drawer, we can pro-
crastinate a little longer. On the refrigerator, it's in our
face and reminds us daily that we need to do something

about the obligation we're avoiding. If it's in the drawer, we can say later that the date just simply escaped us. If it's on the refrigerator, we eventually have to face the fact that someone's waiting for an answer. We need to pick up the phone, send a note, agree to go or—and this is the worst—come up with a made-up excuse.

Several years ago, I lived in a town full of Christian women. At least, that's how it seemed to me. There were Bible studies and Christian women's clubs and even Christian aerobics. Most of all, there seemed always to be support. The day would grow dark, but we had our friends. Our husbands might travel, but other women in the same boat would call and say, "Let's do lunch or coffee." In such a setting, women were for the most part aboveboard. Not once in the two years I had lived there did I hear one woman suggest she might have to "make an excuse" for something. Not until the clothing party, that is—and not until I discovered one day that a neighbor was no longer speaking to me.

Because the winters can be long in the northernmost parts of this country, we women were always looking for one thing or another to keep us busy. Sometimes we'd fill our days with coffee get-togethers. Other days, we'd plan a luncheon or even a crafting party. The women who knew how to embroider might get together as well. Any and every invitation could sound like a day in Disneyland when the temperatures had dropped to forty-five below zero and the snow had drifted to our kneecaps. When our husbands were traveling or working long hours, our homes felt not only cold but empty. So, when a clothing party was suggested, everyone was game. We'd seen samples of the lovely things to be shown there; a club speaker had given us a taste of the finery that would be offered for sale when she'd spoken to our larger group.

Several women had jumped at the chance to sign up for parties held in their homes. It worked like a Tupperware party; you invited your friends, the demonstrator showed her wares, women bought clothing—or at least the hostess hoped that they would do so—and then at least one of the attendees was expected to agree to a party in her home. And on it went. Showing, selling, signing up to hold yet another party.

When these chains begin, there are dozens of women eager and ready to do lots of buying. But once several parties have been held in a small town? Buyers begin to feel short on both cash and enthusiasm. The week Carolyn agreed to hold a party, that's exactly where most of the others were—though not one woman had come straight out and said so. Instead, Carolyn began to hear from one and then another, "Oh, yes, I would love to come" or "You bet I'll be there, and thank you so much for asking." But the night of her party it became an entirely different story. Not only did the women who'd said yes not show, they didn't call. Not to say, "I'm sorry," and not even to make an excuse—because, they said later, they'd each thought all the others would be there; each woman thought she would be the only non-attendee.

I know this because I didn't attend. In my case—this time—I had a legitimate excuse; we would be out of state. But I hadn't called to say so, and my neighbor quit speaking to me.

"What in the world?" I asked one friend and then another. No, I hadn't made it to the clothing party, but why had Carolyn walked right on by me at the store? Why, when I'd waved across the road, had she turned on her heel and gone back into her home? Why, when I'd seen her recently at a luncheon meeting, had she chosen someplace else to sit? And why was I beginning to notice she not only avoided me but all the others, too?

"The party," a mutual friend said one morning when we were walking.

"The party?"

Alice nodded. "None of us, it turns out, showed up."

"None? You mean—?"

"That's right. Each of us thought the others would go, so we all stayed home." She shook her head. "All," she said, "except for the clothing person . . . and our former friend, the hostess."

"Oh, no," I groaned, imagining the baking and setting up a table and making all that coffee—and then the demonstrator sets up—and no one else ever shows.

"Well, we'd been to so many," my friend said.

"But someone should have said that."

Alice shrugged.

"Everyone should have said that, in fact," I said. If they'd told her up front that they couldn't or wouldn't be attending, she'd never have gone to all of that work—or been embarrassed.

"You've never done anything like that?" Alice asked.

This time, I just nodded. She was right, of course, because I could remember several instances when I'd said I would be somewhere, but then I hadn't made an appearance at all. There had been days and nights when I'd decided I was simply too bushed, the day had been too long already, the others would be sufficient cover for me.

I'd like to say the story had a happy ending, but it didn't really. Yes, many of the women continued to meet in their large group on a monthly basis—and sometimes Carolyn attended—but the camaraderie never again felt the same, and our Bible study attendance—in a few short weeks—began to fall off. There was always that feeling that something akin to a wall had grown between us. We each tried in our awkward way to mend the fence, but when Carolyn moved to another town, none of us could actually say we'd done our best to make up for letting her down—in part, because Carolyn was too angry and hurt while the rest of us were too ashamed.

Three days ago, a friend called to ask if I could meet her for lunch, and I knew without even thinking twice that I would be too busy. Still, I wanted to say yes because I needed lunch. I wanted to tell her I'd be there, because she's an old, old friend, and our getting together almost never happens. But my workload had become heavy, and I had a deadline to meet—and I needed to stay close to my own home. The first words on the tip of my tongue, however, were "I'd love that!" and "I think I can . . . just maybe."

Those were my thoughts *before* Carolyn came to mind—and I looked directly at my good friend—a friend I didn't want to risk losing. "I can't," I said, "but I sure would like to." So far, I'd told the truth. "It's my workload," I said. "I'm up to my eyeballs with busy." This was not an excuse; I'd told the truth. "But," I said, reminding myself not to step over the line and not to start giving any false impressions, "if you're not busy once this deadline is behind me, maybe we could try for lunch a little later?"

My friend smiled and nodded. "Sure, no problem," she said.

No problem, no hard feelings, no excuses that would let my friend down or trip me up the next time I had to face her.

"Love does no harm to its neighbor. Therefore love is the fulfillment of the law" (Rom. 13:10).

Love and being a friend and neighbor. Hand-in-hand, face-to-face, taking walks together and honest talking. Excuse-making has no place in such give-and-take connections. Today, if a friend calls to ask if I am busy? I still am, and I'll need to say so. Today I'll remember Carolyn, and I'll speak the truth to my friend.

33

Riding the Metro
with Morgan Grace

"I tell you the truth, unless you change and become like little children, you will never enter the kingdom of heaven."

Matthew 18:3

Unlike my nine-year-old granddaughter, I was feeling burdened by everything. My husband's work, mine, our household expenses, repairs that hadn't been expected, even a friend's walking through divorce. I'd wake up heavyhearted and go to bed feeling the same. I'd pray, but then I'd wonder if all my breath had been wasted. I'd ask others to pray, then doubt that they would.

"Stress," the doctor had said; I needed to do something for it. The something could be a pill, if that's what I would agree to. But I would not.

"I'll work this out," I said. I wasn't interested in additional tests or pills. If I had the faith of a mustard seed, I could cope.

But the following week, I wasn't coping. Not until my granddaughter called to ask if I would take her to the Children's Museum did I begin to turn around.

The turning began with a ride on the Metro into downtown D.C. I'd picked up Morgan Grace at her mom's apartment; we'd walked the several blocks to the closest stop and, if it worked out, we would transfer a couple of times or more—simply because my granddaughter liked to do that.

"Mom-Mom!" she kept saying as she skipped along next to me, "if we have time, maybe we could ride on *all* the lines!"

All? As in green line, orange line, red, and yellow, and blue? I didn't think so, but I didn't say so. The grin on her face and the way she bounced while she talked made it clear I'd probably end up doing whatever she wanted to do, because my name is "Mom-Mom" and because she's my Morgan Grace.

We did the transferring we had to do, and then we climbed the stairs that would put us in front of Union Station and the shops and the café where Morgan Grace picked what she wanted to eat (nothing her mother would have selected for her). Then we started walking. We'd been told by one of the café owners that our museum would be straight through the station to the other street. Only it wasn't. Out-of-town buses had lined up where we'd thought we would walk; we'd been forced to make our way back inside again. Maybe if we took a certain escalator, Morgan Grace said, we could get there. And we tried, but that also turned out to be a dead end.

"Okay, then," my granddaughter said, a delighted grin rounding her face, "let's just try going back there." She pointed to the farthest end of the station.

I couldn't help but smile. First, she'd loved the jerking movement of the train, and now she was actually looking forward to a hike! This child was *not* going to let anything discourage her or ruin the plans we'd made together. She'd decided this would be a good day, so it was. Period. Not only that, she had her hand in my hand; she had no fear of becoming lost, no reason to feel afraid.

And so it went. She'd think about it a bit; she'd point to a place on our map; we'd agree that this could be it, so we'd go—and end up exactly where we'd begun. Still, my optimistic granddaughter—whose legs were much shorter than mine—continued to grin. "This is fun!" she said. She liked going all around Union Station and up and down the escalators and stairs again.

But I did not; my legs ached; I'd begun to experience a pain in my neck and back.

"Mom-Mom," Morgan Grace said, tipping her head to make it appear she was scolding, "you *can* do this."

I could? My legs didn't think so, and neither did my head.

"Just think!" she sang. "Pretty soon we're just going to go up over a hill or something and around behind a building somewhere and there it will be!" Her laughter made all of this walking for nothing seem like a treasure hunt.

Meanwhile, I'd found a tourist's map on the floor. On it I could see the Children's Museum, but I didn't see how we could possibly get there from here.

Morgan Grace, on the other hand, did see. "We'll just go right through here." She pointed with her pretty fingers. "And then we'll turn around there." She was still pointing, but now she was also watching me. "You see?"

I saw that it was going to be several blocks before we found what we were seeking. I also saw that I was worn out already, while my granddaughter had become a portrait of joy. But, once we finally found it and we were inside the Children's Museum, Morgan Grace's enthusiasm began to rub off on me. I hadn't picked up on the simple joy of riding the Metro into town or hanging onto a center pole with one hand, but sitting down in the miniature chairs in a frivolously arranged room, I touched all the items on the tables marked "Please Touch." I listened while the docents explained amazing displays. I hummed with my granddaughter when she'd begin to hum. And I colored. I colored on papers and sort of smudged things around with my fingertips in clay. I ate a Happy Meal, shared my toy with Morgan Grace—and laughed for the first time in days, because I felt like a kid again.

Two weeks later, my husband came home with the news that he'd been passed over for the one promotion he'd wanted. The one that would move us home, the one we'd prayed for and waited for. The one chance that probably wouldn't come along again.

Watching Scotty's face, I felt there was nothing I could say or do. I longed to make him see that surely there was somewhere else, something else he could be. On the other hand, I felt down as well.

The next day was a Saturday. "Let's go for a walk," I said.

A walk? Scotty didn't think so; he had mowing and yard work to do.

"No," I said, "we need to walk." A friend had mentioned a park we'd never been to. "Let's go there. We can walk through the woods. It isn't yet officially open, so there won't be many people." At the park, we would have dozens and dozens of acres to ourselves.

Scotty shrugged. We could walk, but his heart would not be in it.

For half an hour, we walked without saying a word. Around us there were rainbows of birds, and overhead the sky was warm and blue. Still, like a heavy drape, a sadness covered my husband and sloped his shoulders. Silently praying, I asked that God dispel the doubts that Scotty was having.

Not until we had entered a clearing with willow trees and had come around a corner of bushes and brush did we spot the teeter-totter.

"Scotty!" I exclaimed, remembering the last time I'd dangled from one of these things with Morgan Grace. "Let's do it!"

"Do *what?*" Scotty frowned.

"Teeter-totter," I said.

The look on his face made it clear he thought I'd really lost it. I'm not quite five and a half feet tall, while he's nearly six-foot-three. The difference in our heights and weights, he began to explain—

"I don't care," I said, thinking I sounded exactly like Morgan Grace. "I want to; I really want to. Please?"

Scotty was shaking his head, but he looked tempted.

So, with just that little bit of encouragement and refusing to give up, I grabbed his hand again and began tugging him toward the balanced board. Pointing to the end sticking straight up, I suggested he go there. I'd straddle the seat nearest the ground. He didn't immediately give in, but pretty soon—and after he'd made certain no one else was watching—he agreed. Not only that, we hadn't been on that teeter-totter for more than seconds, when my husband began to grin. The grin began to grow as his speed increased. Pretty soon, he was pushing off, popping higher and higher, ascending and descending and ascending with his knees bent and his boots on the ground, while I dangled my legs at my end. His laughter filling the playground, he looked like the young man I'd married, the one who hadn't been passed over for a promotion, the one who hadn't actually cared.

We'd played for nearly an hour when we agreed it was time to go home. "But," Scotty said, "we need to do these things more often."

"Teeter-totters?" I said.

"Play," he said, laughing. "We need to be kids sometimes, Babe." Like Morgan Grace, we needed to express some optimism once in a while. We needed to celebrate the simple joys, needed to remember how very blessed we were.

We needed—every now and then—to behold the world through a child's eyes.

34

The Whiner

But godliness with contentment is great gain.

1 Timothy 6:6

We call it whining, but God doesn't. He calls it grumbling—and he hates it. If you don't believe this, look at what he says in his Word: "And do not grumble, as some of them did—and were killed by the destroying angel" (1 Cor. 10:10).

Killed? I was *only* speaking my mind, saying how I felt about a thing. Like the time we'd driven through our former neighborhood and lingered in front of the beautiful home we'd built—the one we'd been forced to vacate because of a career decision. The home on the hill that we currently owned was a nice enough house, but it didn't begin to compare with what we'd lost. And how about my complaints against the people who'd returned another of my stories when I'd worked so hard? How would they feel if they were on the receiving end of some of these rejections? And the woman who'd cut me off in traffic? Did she understand how close we'd both come to having a terrible accident?

Worse, did no one understand that my being snubbed by those neighborhood women who met for lunch had set me back for weeks? Not only that, I'd needed a new outfit for a wedding, but then I'd gone to shop for something special and discovered the prices were beyond me. Sure, there was a dress that would work, and it had fallen within my budget, but why did I always have to settle for what I didn't actually want? And about my body? "I wish I had another one, Lord. Just look at the shape my shape is in!" And another thing—about my hair. Why couldn't it be curly?

Maybe you don't grumble about sticky floors and handles or the way your husband leaves his dresser drawers open by half an inch or how rudely you were treated when you called to report a problem with your newly purchased television. Maybe your children's teachers have all treated your offspring as if they were their very own. Maybe you've never stood in line for more than an hour for the tickets you'd need for your entire family only to be told they'd sold out.

But I have, and I'd decided I had a right to own my anger. The world was a mess. No one cared anymore. I'd had it with the human race and with my husband's habits and with the way that repairmen never really repaired, and you almost never came home with what you thought you'd paid for.

"It's grumbling, though," a friend said to me one morning. "And God says he really hates it."

Digging in my heels and drawing on my German constitution, I told her I didn't care. His Word had been written before the telemarketer had even been invented! Obviously, he hadn't foreseen how annoying people could be or that the things we would pay too much for would all turn out to be shabby, unhealthy, or flawed. And what about all the disappointments regarding the people we'd grown up with? What about thinking you could turn your back, but you could not? What about the weather? Did he understand that some days when the clouds were too gray or the sun too hot we simply deteriorated? Hadn't I read recently where a man and his wife—with more money than they knew what to do with—were buying yet another house abroad, when we were finding it difficult to make the payments on our single, lackluster home? Movie stars living disgraceful lives were being treated as idols and heroes—while those of us who worked long hours for short pay remained faceless.

"I'm sorry you feel that way," my friend said, "but God has his reasons and ways; and grumbling *is* something he hates." She also made an attempt at telling me how much worse off other people were, but I hadn't really listened.

The following week, packing for a trip to Nevada with my husband, I considered my friend's last word—and decided to forget it. She didn't understand; she'd been married for years and years to the only guy she had ever dated. They had a lovely family, a lovely home, and money would never be a problem. She had her health and was surrounded by the friends that she'd grown up with; and if she needed something, she simply bought it.

"No," I said, snapping all the latches on my luggage, "she doesn't know." She thought that just because I often got to travel with my husband, I was blessed. She believed, because my husband provided a better-than-average income, that I should be singing praises. She'd said more than once that whether or not I became a "successful" writer, God had called me to do what I did, and all that he asked was that I be faithful.

On our flight, I continued to think about the habit my friend said I'd developed. "With your mouth," she said, "you are whining."

So?

"So, you're not only going against what God has taught us, but you're bringing yourself down as well."

That part was true; I'd seen it coming for some time. I'd murmur a word, and sure enough, before long I felt not better but worse. I'd grumble about how ill-behaved a grocery clerk could be, and the next time I'd find myself in her line, she'd act as if she'd never seen me. I'd groused about having too small a house, and the house had grown smaller and smaller. I'd even purchased a poster for my office wall that warned, "Snap out of it!"—but the murmuring had only grown worse.

But now we were on our way to a meeting in Reno, and I was going to treat myself to some sights I hadn't yet seen. I was also going to do some shopping.

The morning after we arrived, Scotty headed for his meetings, and I headed for the exit from our hotel. Wending my way between the gambling machines and the poor souls who'd become addicted, I thought how blessed I was that my husband had never once been tempted. Passing through the bar that stayed open all night, I thanked God for a husband who took walks with me in the evening and came home each day from work— a husband who'd never once gambled or otherwise squandered his paycheck. Entering a lobby where women who'd been making change all night waited for transportation, I said a prayer of thanks that I didn't have to work if I didn't want to and that God had sufficiently provided. "But," I started to say—when I spotted a gift shop and on a shelf above the proprietor's head a white mug. On the mug was a red circle with a slash across it—the symbol for "No" or "Stamp Out!"—and behind the symbol was one word: "Whining."

197

"No Whining" the red, black, and white mug said—and I began to smile.

"I have to have that," I said, stopping where a blonde-headed woman counted her daily change.

"The what?"

"The mug," I said. I pointed.

"Oh," she said, smiling now and reaching around over her shoulder to retrieve the mug from the shelf. "I'd sure like to see the face of the person you're buying this for," she added.

"I'm buying it for me," I said—as the woman set my mug down.

"For you?"

I nodded. "For me."

"Well," she said—and then she laughed. "I guess you know yourself pretty well."

"Yes, I do," I said, laughing with her. "I finally do."

35

You Mud, You Tape— and You Keep Going

Let us not become weary in doing good, for at the proper time we will reap a harvest if we do not give up.

Galatians 6:9

I couldn't keep writing. I'd worked nearly eighteen years, but still I hadn't experienced real success. "I'm working on a novel," I'd said in this year's Christmas letter—and last year's and the year before that. It had my heart; I was full of longing—"But I have only pages upon pages *and* frustration," I'd written a writer friend. "Really," I said later, sitting on Scotty's lap, "I gave it my best. I tried, no one can say I did not." But to keep going when I didn't honestly know what I was doing? To work every day, every year, and to see my nearly nonexistent income consumed by first one and then another expense? Maybe it was time to give up.

The following week, my husband announced he would be quitting his job. "Retiring," he said. Everyone figured it had everything to do with his age, but it didn't. "My wife has supported every one of my career decisions . . . traipsed from state to state with me all these years," he wrote in his final mailing to other agency employees. "It's her turn. She's a wonderful writer; it's time I supported her."

Next, he announced that I was to do no more laundry; he was capable of running a dryer and washer. "Cooking, too," he said. "It won't be gourmet; it'll be meat and potatoes"—but I wasn't to lift a finger. "You go upstairs and type." These other jobs would now be his. Before long, he'd added grocery shopping.

Still, with this gift of time, I couldn't seem to make myself focus. Flowers on my desk needed replacing; the dining room was dusty; the cat had licked smudges on all the windows and even on the French doors. "And the vacuuming," I said. "At least let me—"

"Excuses," Scotty said. "You're stalling."

He was right; with nearly five hundred manuscript pages in random stacks around my room, I'd become overwhelmed. Even filing felt beyond me—until the day I wandered down into "his basement."

Although my spouse retired from a desk job, he knows how to use tools; he grew up on a ranch—and he'd decided he needed a project. If he finished our lower level with a full bath, family room, and laundry room, we could make some money when we were ready to sell.

He began by framing in the duct work with thin slivers of wood beside slivers of wood beside others. "I don't *want* to go down there," I'd see written on his face in the morning. But within weeks the framing was complete. "Next," he said, "I'll deal with the wiring, insulation, and drywall."

If you've never worked with drywall, you don't know—as I did not—it's heavy. Only once could a friend come to help. That's the day we discovered you couldn't get 4 x 8 sheets down our stairwell, and Scotty had no choice but to pull back living room carpet, remove two wide boards from the floor, and push the drywall through a hole he'd create in the floor.

Next, he rented a mechanical lift and pushed, shoved, and wrestled it to his work space where he would also be surrounded (and slowed down) by a Nordic Trak, an inflatable boat, and boxes of Christmas books and dishes. He never said, "I love doing this." He never even said, "like." It was simply a commitment he'd made, a job he'd made up his mind to do well.

And he did. From morning until evening, he'd work with his shoulders and arms aching so badly they'd burn, and then he'd lie on the floor while I'd run the massager over his back. Week after week, with his fingers beginning to lose any sense of feeling and with one hand growing so much larger it looked as if it belonged to some other man.

Finally, after what seemed like months of lifting and securing, he completed the project with the drywall. Now he would apply three layers of mud and three of tape—skimming and smoothing after every layer—even though I'd repeatedly say, "Why? It looks fine; no one's going to see *little* flaws."

Still he kept on going. "I've come this far," he'd say. So last week while I typed rewrites upstairs in my office, Scotty began preparing the walls with what they call a primer—and a neighbor came by. A sister-in-law, the neighbor said, was interested in buying our home.

"She's especially interested in the finished basement," he told us.

Yesterday, while Scotty applied a second coat of paint, a second neighbor stopped by. She knows how hard

Scotty's working. "How conscientious he is," she says. In two weeks, could she bring her brother with her? She believes he will purchase our home. Add to that a note from strangers who would also like us to consider an offer, and I now understand that my husband's perseverance—even when he hasn't felt like persevering—*will* be rewarded.

And so will mine—and yours.

Writing isn't easy; housework isn't easy; raising children isn't easy, either. But what about finishing a basement when a man's been behind a desk for thirty years? "It won't get done by itself," Scotty said yesterday morning. Whether I thought he worked too hard or not, he needed to finish what he'd begun. It wasn't clear to him in the beginning that he could pull this off. From time to time, he made mistakes and had to tear something out or start all over again. There were days when he'd read the books on "How To"—but the words had gone over his head. Those days, he'd driven to the local home-improvement center with his growing list of problems.

There have also been days when I thought I couldn't deal with one more housewife dilemma, days when even making it to a car pool felt impossible. Nowadays I have mornings when I don't *want* to go to my home office desk or keyboard. There are even more days—though I now have 1500 pages—when I still can't envision a finished novel, when I feel I have nothing but fragments and loosely knit ends. On the other hand, there *is* a beginning; it's when I began. The middle is there as well. The end will come when the work is finished, when I've primed, refined, and touched up—just as my husband has prepared those walls with framing, wallboard, and paint for going on one full year. Like Scotty, I've had questions, and I've had to make lists, sought help from any handy expert I could corner. I've also had to discover by trial and error how to frame in my work and how many layers I'll need of yet another character or color. I'm also learning that a hit-or-miss job isn't going to bring the buyers. Buyers come when the work is done and done well.

This morning—certain I couldn't do another line of dialogue—I took two stout mugs of our favorite coffee downstairs. One for me and one for Scotty. "You don't have to keep going over that door frame," I said. How many times did he think he had to touch up? "It's good enough; the lights will be low; we'll hang pictures on every wall."

My husband smiled.

Over the top of my coffee, I smiled, too. "Back upstairs?" I said.

"Back upstairs."

"You're going to do this until it's right, right?"

"Yup," my husband said, laughing. "And so will you."

"And so will I," I said, returning his laughter. Then, taking two stairs in one bound, I headed back to *my* workplace—knowing I might not yet know where I'm to place all the people and pages, but also knowing one thing's certain: Whether we're gardening, typing, or sending a firstborn off to school for the first time, the job doesn't get done by itself. But once we've written "The End" and we've done the best that we can?

The joy, the sense of satisfaction . . . and maybe even the buyers . . . will come.

36

I Have No Money, Father

For if the willingness is there, the gift is acceptable according to what one has, not according to what he does not have.

2 Corinthians 8:12

"Father, I have no money," I said one morning during my quiet time. *No money?* That wasn't exactly the truth. If you looked at my husband's income and our home and all the lovely things in it, we were doing more than well. But I hadn't personally earned or seen a paycheck for my own work in a very long time—and I wanted to know why. Why, when I believed God had called me, couldn't I make the kind of money paid a Grisham or a Danielle Steele? *Because I don't write nearly so well,* was the first thought that immediately came to mind. The second "thought" was even more disturbing.

"Give $100.00 to Lisa," I heard.

Give $100.00 to Lisa? Wait just one minute. Had God not heard *my* heart's cry? Did he not understand we were talking about *my* need? Of course I wanted to help my youngest daughter, but my husband and I had been helping her for a long time, and now she was helping herself. No, I didn't want her or our granddaughter to go without, but give another $100.00? From money that came only on occasion, though I wrote daily and pushed myself very hard?

From my money. There was no doubting I had heard the Lord. So I wrote a check for $100.00 from an account that could support only one or two more of these gifts before my bank would be sending me a note.

I didn't tell my husband or my daughter; I just wrote it and mailed it and, several days later, I answered the phone.

"Mom . . ." My daughter was weeping. It wasn't easy for her to express what she felt, but the money had come at the very time when she'd just heard they'd be raising the fee for our granddaughter's daycare, and their rent had been increased, and now she'd had to go in for unexpected dental work. Stretching her single-mother paycheck was becoming nearly impossible.

I assured her I was happy to do it—and, hearing her joy, I meant it. This felt good. Not only that, I kept to myself, I could now go to God and remind him about his Word regarding pressed down and overflowing. Wasn't that how it went? I'd give to someone, and then he'd give back to me?

On my knees, I said I'd been writing for fourteen years, and I still barely made enough to cover the cost of envelopes, and now I'd given away $100.00—

"Send $50.00 to Verda," I heard.

My friend Verda needed $50.00? She and her husband were missionaries, but didn't their denomination meet their needs? *"Fifty* dollars, Lord?"

205

That afternoon, I wrote a check for $50.00, but this was making no sense at all. I understood that my friend wrote for magazines and papers that paid very little, but I also had a calling, didn't I? Hadn't I given up a teaching job to write? And hadn't I been receiving checks you couldn't call real pay?

It took several weeks for my note to find El Salvador and another week for Verda's to make its way to me. "What a surprise!" she wrote. "Thank you very, very much. I used the money to buy a new printer. A friend in Illinois gave me $100.00, and you gave me $50.00, and the printer cost $150.00. Isn't God good! Thank you for obeying him."

"Thank you for obeying him," my friend had written. "Mom, I love you very much," my daughter had said.

Surveying my study in our lovely home, I flicked dust from one of my two printers. Once upon a time, I—like my youngest—had also been a single mother, but today a godly husband would walk through our back door, and he'd hug me, and after dinner he would help with dishes. We'd go for our evening walk, and together we would share our day and prayer.

"I have plenty, Father," I said. And it was true. No more whining. God had already richly blessed me.

But two weeks later, a check came. A publisher was paying me $70.00 for a reprint; it had cost me only postage to submit it. One week later, that same publisher wrote to say he'd accepted a second story. For this one, they would pay me $10.00 more than for the first; their $80.00 check would be mailed that afternoon. My $150.00 had been returned to me—but staring at the two checks several days later and preparing my deposit slip, I finally understood that more dollars would never again completely satisfy.

Nothing would ever again compare with my friend's "Thank you very, very much" or with my daughter's joy.

37

With Our Focus on God

And Elisha prayed, "O LORD, open his eyes so he may see." Then the LORD opened the servant's eyes, and he looked and saw the hills full of horses and chariots of fire all around Elisha.

2 Kings 6:17

We'd sold our house in Virginia on a Wednesday. Three days later, on a Saturday, we'd flown to Montana to shop for another home. The following evening, on Mother's Day, we'd written a check, signed a Buy-Sell Agreement, and prepared to fly back to pack boxes for yet another move. Yes, we'd made some pretty serious decisions rather quickly, and friends had wondered if we might have been better off staying put in our Virginia home. Still, we'd prayed, and we were certain we were going in the right direction. Furthermore, the Montana house had looked spotless. We'd even hired a home inspector, and he said it was okay. Not only that, the time *seemed* right. Seemed, that is, until I began to experience what felt like an emotional decline full of doubt, and then we moved in, and we began to wonder . . . as we also began to encounter first one and then another "surprise."

We hadn't been in our new home one full day before we discovered a serious leak under a basement sink. "No real problem though," Scotty said. He could fix it. However, just one day after he'd fixed the basement leak, I'd filled a bucket with sudsy ammonia to wipe off a "couple of small spots on the wall"—and discovered that instead of wiping *off* spots, I was *creating* them! The more I wiped, the dirtier the walls became!

Calling down the stairs to where my husband had been trying not only to bring order in the storage room but to cage our cat, I said I needed help—which was an understatement. I wanted to shriek, "We've bought ourselves a pigsty!" Instead, I said, "We'll be needing a cleaning crew."

As he topped the stairs, stared, and shook his head, Scotty admitted I hadn't exaggerated this time. Not only were the walls thick with something that looked exactly like soot, but the ceilings were coated, too. "I don't want you doing any more scrubbing," he said. He would finish what I'd begun.

But three scrubbings later and with the walls still not clean, water from a shower head began to trickle down a bathroom wall.

At first, Scotty felt certain he not only had the tools but the expertise to fix such a simple thing. The expertise, we soon discovered, he did have. The tools, he did not—which meant several more trips into town to visit with not one but three "experts" in the plumbing business. It would also mean hauling our toiletries and clothing down to the guest room on the lower level, because our bath would be out of commission for we didn't know how long—and because my husband would be cutting a hole in a freshly scrubbed wall.

Not three days later, the rains came . . . and water began to flow down our driveway and under the entire garage door to where we'd stacked our unpacked clothing and household goods.

"I'll deal with that next." My husband, looking more than a little weary, ran his hand through his thinning hair.

But this morning we decided the garage will have to wait. The refrigerator's begun to act up. The motor isn't turning off.

"Don't worry," Scotty said, while we were having breakfast and figuring a way to fix this problem, too.

"So did we make a mistake buying this house?" I wanted to know. Should we have built our own as we'd originally planned? On the other hand, hadn't God— even in seemingly small ways—made it clear he was in the lead? And even if I did feel weary and was wishing we'd never come to this place, hadn't we been blessed with the renewing of old friendships here? Hadn't we also experienced great joy as we'd watched each daily sunrise on "our" mountains and trees?

"Focus," Scotty said this afternoon over lunch. "We just need to keep our eyes on God *and* on what we're doing." We couldn't keep wondering if and why. There was no point in looking back—and listening to my husband, I remembered a surgery several years ago.

I'd opted to stay awake. I'd recover more quickly, my doctor had explained. I would go home feeling less frail if they didn't have to put me under. But then the surgery began, a surgery that would take several hours, a surgery that would require the use of hammers, chisels, and saws. I knew my doctor knew what he was doing, but suddenly I did not. He'd taken a great deal of time for my reassuring, but still I was afraid. Every time I'd hear him run his saw, I'd wonder if my bones would ever again grow. When I'd hear him apply a chisel, I'd imagine part of my foot falling off, and then I'd tense up and think that maybe my heart would stop.

These were my thoughts, that is, until a nurse at the foot of the operating table came to where I could see and hear her. "Just focus on me," she was saying in a voice as soft as a mother's and pulling out a stool and sitting down. "I'm going to watch the monitors from here," she said, taking and squeezing my hand. "So you just look only at me," she said again—and then she began to tell me about her children and to ask me all about mine, and as I focused on the words she spoke, I began to rest.

Five minutes ago, I left my tiny home office and walked into our master bath. I'd been listening to the hammers and the chisels Scotty had been using on the pipes and wall. I'd tried not to think about it, but he'd been working far too hard.

"Well," I said, "how's it going?"

Scotty shook his head.

"Not good?"

"The tool they sold me isn't working."

"What are we going to do?" I asked.

"I don't know." He shook his head again. "Call a professional plumber?"

Call a professional plumber? We'd now discovered there was also soot in the carpet and, when he'd checked again in the front yard, Scotty had found he'd be replacing six sprinkler heads. Worse than all of that, he'd been on the roof, spotted shingles that had evidently blown off sometime in a wind, but the former owner had only nailed them back down. Under those shingles, the tar paper had split. If we didn't get that taken care of, the attic was going to be covered with rain.

"We bought the wrong house, didn't we?" I said. I hadn't wanted to consider *or* mention this possibility again; we were in no position emotionally or financially to make yet another move.

Scotty shrugged.

"It would make you think that we had though, wouldn't it?"

"Babe . . ." Scotty said, putting his hand over mine. "Remember what we said about needing to focus on God?" This time he was looking directly at me. "We prayed about this move; we asked him to show us how and where—and now we're here." It was as plain and simple as that for him. We'd prayed, we'd asked, and we could trust that God had been faithful. He was our bottom line. Everything we thought we saw—everything we half suspected? None of it compared to what God had promised in his Word. We weren't to focus on the problems we *could* see; we were to trust that *he* would provide. Period.

Nodding, I closed my eyes . . . and allowed myself to remember . . . that last night, long after the neighbors had all gone to bed, I'd been standing at my open office window not only looking at the mountains but delighting in their fragrance when the Lord had spoken in a whisper to my spirit. "Make this the home you've always wanted," he'd said.

Make this the home? "Lord," I'd whispered, looking at the sky and noting how very close the stars seemed. "How?"

And then I'd "heard" the only two words I needed. "Trust *me*."

Turning back again to my diligent husband and friend, I nodded. "You're right," I said. "I need to focus *only* on him."

Our problems with this house would be temporary, but God is not . . . and never will be.

38

No Argument with God

There is nothing wrong with swimming—except when God wants you walking on the water.

Don Basham
New Wine, November 1981

My husband's an adventurer; I suspect he always has been. But do I feel the same about risks? I do not. Still, for months now, he'd been talking about white-water rafting—and not just for him but for me.

"Babe, just think," he'd said.

I had been thinking; I'm a writer. I have a vivid imagination; I could easily predict how "thrilling" such a caper could be.

"We'll be perfectly safe," Scotty insisted. There would be expert guides, people who floated rivers for a living. "Why can't you just trust me?"

Trust him? Wasn't this the same character who'd tricked me into learning to downhill ski on a sheer-faced

Utah mountain? Wasn't this the guy who'd signed me up for the pack trip with two strings of mules in a snowstorm on switchback trails—without mentioning that I'd be setting up a hunting camp for and with a bunch of men? And what about the time he sweet-talked me to the top of a three-foot-wide Montana ridge where I couldn't see all the way to the bottom?

Still, I love him, and he can be so convincing. "Okay," I said, staring at his brochures and photos and wondering if that was elation or fright on the faces of the rafters who'd signed on last year. "I'll do it," I said—but I would not be glad.

We'd float the New River in West Virginia. It would be beautiful; he knew how much I loved the hills. What my beloved didn't happen to mention? This rafting company offered five floats. Class One: "the scenic cruise." Class Five: "Do the kids know where your wills are hidden?" Scotty had signed me up for Class Five.

The ride to the river was lovely; Scotty hadn't stretched the truth about the hills. I did wonder though, as we'd boarded the bus and discovered the other floaters were younger than my own kids. Because I'm two years older than my spouse, I'd be the only passenger five years beyond fifty years old. God had his reasons, I supposed, but couldn't he have created me just a little later?

"Scotty," I said, pinching my husband's hand. "Are you sure?"

He grinned.

"What did you do, take out life insurance on me?"

This time, he laughed.

At the landing where we met up with our rower, I pushed my silvered hair up under the mandatory helmet. Not only were the passengers all younger, our pint-sized guide didn't look old enough to be out without her mother—another reminder that life had passed me by and that I really hadn't done a lot of living.

"You'll love this," Scotty whispered in my ear as he checked the buckle on my jacket.

The start of the float wasn't half bad. Scenic, actually. Maybe Scotty was right; maybe I would become grateful.

From there, however, it was all downhill. Curves I hadn't seen coming, up and over rocks, stretches that went in seconds from exhilarating to, "I'm out of here!" Around us, several inflatables had flipped! In another boat, one man who'd nearly been lost in whorls of furious water was shrieking that he would *not* be climbing back in!

But behind me Scotty was laughing, and once again I made up my mind I would enjoy myself, as well. Hadn't God made the rivers and the mountains? Hadn't we prayed this morning? Didn't I trust him? Well, sometimes I did, and sometimes I didn't—but the river really was thrilling, and there were calm places where a person could catch her breath. Besides, I hadn't been thrown out once, and I was paddling on the left when our guide yelled, "Paddle left!" When told to, I also paddled right. Okay, so this would be like our previous adventures. At the end of the day, Scotty would hug me and say how proud he was, and I'd tell him he was crazy and that I loved him, and I'd feel proud, too.

We'd been on the river for two hours when our guide pointed to a rock taller than our two-story house. Somewhere around back, she was saying, a person could scramble out of the boat and climb up. "But you'll have to be quick!" she shouted. She couldn't spend much time in "the hole." We were to make our way to the top, jump, and swim. Where the waters would begin to be calm again, she'd come pick each of us up.

Nearly everyone wanted to try it—except for Scotty. He loved the idea of the jump, but he can't swim.

A younger man told his wife, "You go!"—but he couldn't deal with the height.

"I want to jump," I mouthed—but had Scotty given me one of his looks? Did he think I couldn't do it?

I'd secured my paddle with both of my hands, when I caught the concern on the face of our guide. Reluctantly, I shook my head. *I'm too old,* I kept to myself. All my life I'd wanted to try things. "But . . ." I shrugged.

It took only seconds for the jumping—while our leader and the three of us still in the boat rowed even harder, and then our frantic guide was shouting how we were to lift the others up over the side as soon as they'd made it back to the boat. "Slip your arms under their armpits!" she yelled. "Grab their straps and jackets!"— and we did, but I couldn't help feeling jealous. "What fun! What a gas! Awesome!" they were shouting. "But it's good you didn't go," one of the girls called to me as she wrapped her arms around her husband. "What an adventure!" she exclaimed—and I looked at Scotty.

"I wanted to go," I said. I'd even prayed . . . but a lot of good that had done me.

Scotty was sorry; he wished he could turn the boat around. "But there will be other times, Babe," he said.

Other times? I wasn't getting any younger; all of my life I'd stayed behind—when I'd wanted to try. All of my life I'd been playing it safe. I wanted to say so, too, but now we were headed for rapids so thunderous he couldn't have heard.

It wasn't until we'd pulled off the river for lunch, that our guide began to tell us about one final thrill. "As exciting as jumping off the rock!" she was declaring, as everyone climbed back in to begin again. We'd be making our way through wider rapids where she'd let us swim if we wanted, but the rocks could be dangerous, the currents tricky. It was critical that we jump when she shouted,

"Jump!" No holding back, no going in early. "Otherwise, you could be trapped under the boat," she said.

"I'm going," I announced—all the while watching the younger passengers watching me and knowing they were wishing I'd stay in the boat with my clearer-thinking husband.

"You sure?" Scotty furrowed his forehead.

"You don't have to!" our guide called from her berth, feverishly rowing and fighting what were becoming enormous onrushes of towering waves and sprays of river water.

"Yeah, *I'm* not," the young husband who hadn't jumped said.

"Maybe you shouldn't," one of the child-faced wives peeped—as I put down my paddle, checked my snaps and buckles, and tightened the strap under my chin. This wasn't going to be another rock-jumping experience with me wishing. I might be the oldest thing on the boat, but I wasn't yet dead. I couldn't help what year I'd been born, but I could do something about not confirming for everyone that I belonged in a rocking chair.

"I'm going," I mouthed, hoping Scotty could read my lips and listening to the sound of what was beginning to feel like an angry river. "I have to," I said.

"Babe, are you sure?" Scotty looked concerned—as our guide struggled to stay upright.

I was sure. "I really want to!" I yelled, as our boat shifted sideways in a circling rush of river.

No one else had said a word, but I could see the stirring rapids coming. Did I remember everything our guide had told us? This wouldn't be any picnic, I remembered—but what had she said about saving ourselves if we got into trouble?

Our boat had picked up speed, and everyone was shrieking at once. We were being washed with water;

the chaos had become alarming, and the thrashing rapids were upon us!

"Did you hear me?" our guide was calling. Hear her what? Couldn't she see I was wearing one of her mandatory helmets? How could she expect—

"Jump!" the others were shouting, nodding at me and one another and either leaping or slipping over the inflated rubber.

She'd yelled for us to jump? Was I too late? Was it my turn? Why couldn't God have given me better hearing? Should I go off the side or the back of this idiot boat?

As soon as I jumped, the waters became colder than I'd expected, and now I'd lost sight of the others! Seven bodies in here with me and I couldn't spot one?

"Don't get in front of the boat," our guide had instructed. "And when you jump, should you get caught—"

A fountain of water had filled my mouth. The rocks had come up to meet my knees. *I should be beside the boat or behind it*, I kept thinking. But it was behind me, and now I was facing up again, and I was being slammed against something sharp.

I thought I heard Scotty and then our guide yell—but now I was on my side and under the water and doing a somersault with something hitting my head! Had the boat run over me? Was I trapped? What had she said about, "If such a thing should happen?" If only I could scream. I grabbed for something, anything—and pressed the palms of my hands against the bottom of the flat boat, all the while knowing I could do nothing.

"If you get caught under the boat," our leader had said, "walk along the bottom with your hands, find the side, and then you'll pop up."

But I couldn't "walk." The boat was moving so fast, and I was moving with it. This was it; life was over.

Jesus . . . Father . . . help me, I silently begged—and suddenly I relaxed . . . as a peace I'd never before known gently washed over me. I took my hands off the boat; I'd had a good life with this husband of mine—even if he had talked me into some things I'd believed I could not do. I had no reason to be angry with anything I'd walked through. No, I hadn't expected to have quite so many challenges, illnesses, and disappointments along the way and, yes, I'd hoped to live a little longer. But the bottom line?

I have no argument with you, Father, I said—and suddenly there was a shift beneath and above me; the boat had taken a turn in the current. I was bobbing to the top of the river and—through eyes full of freezing water—I saw my husband straining to stretch himself out across the edge of the boat and the river to reach his hand to me. And there was the younger man looking pale and, beside him, the pint-sized guide calling my name—and I heard Scotty say, "She's okay, she's okay." My best friend was smiling. "You okay, Babe?" he said.

I nodded and coughed and squeezed my husband's hand. "Okay," I said through teeth that wouldn't stop thrumming.

"You ready for me to pull you up yet?" my husband was asking.

I shook my head.

"You want to keep swimming?" Scotty was giving me a look that said he felt like lifting me up out of that water, but he was also giving me a look that said he understood this swim was something I not only wanted but needed. "The others are just up ahead," he whispered, winking.

"*Grab her!*" our guide was yelling—stretching, now, as far as she could stretch and looking frightened and trying her best to make me take *her* hand.

"Is she all right?" the young man was asking. "Shouldn't we be getting her?"

My soul mate shook his head for the others. "I love you," he mouthed just for me.

"I'm . . . okay," I managed again between spits and coughs of river. Actually, I was more than okay, and both Scotty and I knew it as I began to swim—not so well as I had in my youth but determined to catch up with the laughter erupting from the others.

Really okay, I kept thinking, feeling younger than I had in years and knowing at last what I'd needed to know . . . that I had no argument with God.

Epilogue

I waited patiently for the LORD; he turned to me and heard my cry. He lifted me out of the slimy pit, out of the mud and mire; he set my feet on a rock and gave me a firm place to stand.

Psalm 40:1–2

With our take-out place in our sights and after having fished for hours with nothing to show but sunburn, we still had another stretch of pitching rapids to row through. My face had nearly frozen, my clothing was soaked, and there was frigid, muddy water not only in the river but in our boots and boat. When we'd first spotted the towering bridge above our destination landing, Scotty had pointed out and prepared me for this next series of rocks with the water steep and narrow, but I was still trying to forget an earlier "experience"—and I'd grown afraid.

"Just keep watching the bridge," Scotty said. He couldn't hold my hand. If I didn't think about the convulsing under and around us, I would be okay, he was shouting back over his shoulder. He nodded to where the boat was supposed to go.

"But I'm *not* okay!" I exclaimed. We'd been caught in a lash of backwater, and now my husband was rowing with all the strength a man his age could muster, while the river seemed to have grown even stronger and longer. Within minutes, however, my spouse had pulled our rubber watercraft up onto the shore, and we were laughing and exclaiming that, yes, it had been a little hair-raising for a moment or two, but still there'd been joy, as well.

Life is like that—a series of rapids, a goal in plain view—and we're feeling as if we've finally come through all that we will be asked to come through, when suddenly there appears one last cascade of obstacles and a challenging place with walls on either side, and we're picking our way and rowing with all of our might. We spot the rush of whatever is coming toward us and hear the seeming threats that fill us with fear. And though we're only yards away from where we thought we could pull out, it seems impossible.

But God is our restorer. He has all that's needed to either steer or pull us through. He's never once—though sometimes we've imagined—abandoned me *or* you.

This afternoon I remember talking with a woman who has walked through both cancer and her husband's leaving, one who also nearly lost her son. But she has grown strong in her struggle to keep her head above the water. She hasn't chosen to do so, but God has chosen to show her how. In her flesh, she isn't always happy. In her growing awareness of the God who has always been there for her, she has learned she can also grow.

This afternoon I remember, too, a family of ducks, a grand black swan, and a goose—each one taking cautious quick steps across thinning ice toward a single puddle of water in the middle of a winter pool. I remember thinking that if *they* fell through, *they* were prepared to either fly or swim. But what about us? What if we

Epilogue

approach these chilling situations—either bravely or with caution—these places in our walk where we fear we have entered into a land where the ice is thin? Can we trust that God has already provided for us as well? No, we haven't the wings for such things, and neither do we have webs between our fingers and toes. But just as God had no intention of allowing Peter to drown, neither does he plan to leave us struggling in the deepest parts of our troubles for all eternity. We can "cry unto God most high; unto God that performeth all things for [us]" (Ps. 57:2 KJV)—because he sent his Son a very long time ago so that each of us might come to know the God who is teaching us to trust and to cling.

And when we begin to doubt his loving care for us? Rehearse the things he has done, we are told. Remember all the ways the Lord God has been leading you.

"I will remember the deeds of the LORD," the psalmist wrote. "Yes, I will remember your miracles of long ago. I will meditate on all your works and consider all your mighty deeds" (Ps. 77:11).

He has stretched his arms out for me and for you . . . we have only to take his hand.

Nancy Hoag, an award-winning author, is also a wife, mother of three, and grandmother of five—a grandmother who loves fishing, floating the Yellowstone River, Starbucks Yukon Roast, wildflowers, lemon pie, mountain lakes, and last, but definitely not least, her Montana cowboy, her best friend, the man who not only taught her to try the things she thought she could not accomplish but who offered her unconditional love that she might learn the meaning of trust . . . trusting in herself, in a husband's promise, in God.